## Front Cover

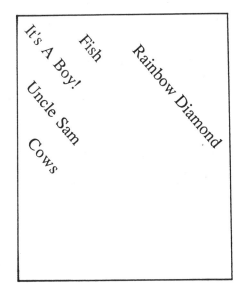

It's A Boy!
Fish
Uncle Sam
Cows
Rainbow Diamond

## Back Cover

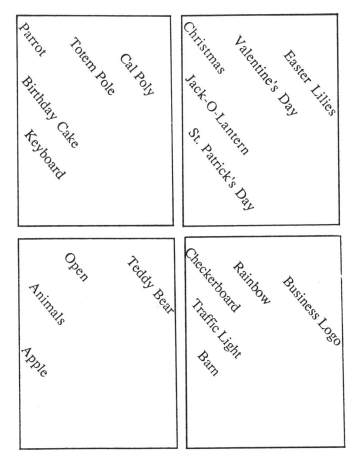

Parrot
Totem Pole
Cal Poly
Birthday Cake
Keyboard

Christmas
Valentine's Day
Easter Lilies
Jack-O-Lantern
St. Patrick's Day

Open
Teddy Bear
Animals
Apple

Checkerboard
Rainbow
Business Logo
Traffic Light
Barn

## Introduction

Many of the construction techniques are the same for all the windsocks in this book. Unless otherwise stated the following general directions apply.

## Materials

Light weight nylon comes in wonderful colors. Taffeta nylon is lightest in weight and has a smooth appearance. Most readymade windsocks are made of taffeta nylon. However, rip stop nylon works well, too, and you may find it more readily available. A big advantage to using rip stop nylon is that the threads woven in for durability also make great guides for cutting and aligning designs. If your favorite fabric store does not carry a wide range of nylon ask that they order it or shop around. It really is not difficult to find and is inexpensive. Sixty inch rip stop is usually $4.98 per yard and 45 inch is $3.98. Wonder Under™ is about $1.69 per yard, plastic tubing (discussed later) is 13¢ per foot and fishing swivels are less than 15¢ each. A spool of nylon string may be something you have around the house. If not, you can find it in hardware stores for under two dollars. The small amount of fabric required for a windsock means you can make one for between $4.00 and $7.00, a considerable savings over the readymade ones.

## Applying Designs

Most of the designs in this book are actual size and can be traced directly. However, some you will need to enlarge. The dimensions will always be given and there are a couple different ways to do this. One simple way is to take the desired pattern to a copy shop (or perhaps you have access to a photo copying machine) and have it enlarged once, twice or more to reach the correct size. Another method is to use a craft projector. This works by projecting the picture you put in onto a wall for tracing. If you do not own one or do not wish to purchase one perhaps you could borrow an opaque projector from a nearby school.

Wonder Under™ by Pellon is a fusible sheet backed by paper. It works beautifully for applying designs of nylon. Designs can be drawn on the paper either before or after fusing it to fabric. Try the permanent press setting on your iron but be sure to experiment on scraps. Preshrink the nylon by ironing all pieces you will be fusing. After cutting out your design peel away paper backing. Do not worry if the nylon fabric bubbles somewhat as you apply the Wonder Under™. After the paper is removed and piece applied these bubbles will disappear. Keep in mind as you trace designs on Wonder Under™ that your final product will actually be a mirror image of that design. For symmetrical designs it will not make a difference but in some instances you may want to turn the design over. It is for this reason that the alphabet letters at the end of this book are reversed.

Machine applique is an attractive and durable method to finish edges of applied designs and it is not difficult if you know a few tricks. If your machine can zigzag you can do machine applique. Find your satin stitch foot (figure 1). Hopefully it will be a clear plastic one. A satin stitch foot is cut away on the bottom to allow the row of stitches to move through easily. Experiment with your machine by turning the top tension down to a lower number so that the top thread is pulled to the back for a neater appearance. Experiment, also,

Figure 1

with stitch length and width. Set length near zero and adjust upward if your fabric does not feed through. The idea is to keep stitches as close together as possible without overlapping. Stitch width should be set somewhere around the middle range; wider stitches make it more difficult to go around curves smoothly.

For a neat applique stitch there are times when you must pivot. When coming to a corner simply stitch to the edge and pivot with the needle down exactly in the corner. See figure 2. Curves are a bit more difficult. Large curves can often be stitched around easily but smaller ones may require several pivots in order to avoid gaps or stitches that slant. Figure 3 shows needle position for pivoting around curves.

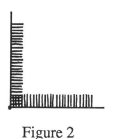

Figure 2

This may look and sound confusing but when you are at your sewing machine it will be very obvious when you need to pivot and where your needle must rest.

Figure 3

Quality thread is important and be sure the top thread and bobbin thread are from the same good quality spool. Less expensive thread leads to big frustration when trying for a neat satin stitch.

One last tip. Never try to applique without a stabilizer behind your background fabric. Tear away stabilizers are found in the interfacing section. They are like a very stiff nonwoven interfacing and they eliminate puckering and slippage when satin stitching. When entire design is appliqued simply tear away stabilizer and discard.

Still having problems? Try a new needle.

Not everyone wants to machine applique designs on windsocks and the good news is that you do not have to. When applied correctly the Wonder Under™ will hold well for many months even in wind and sun. Of course, the satin stitch adds a finished look and is necessary for adding detail to some designs.

## Construction Techniques

The most time consuming part of windsocks is hemming all those streamers. A hemming foot makes a very neat and narrow hem once you learn to use it. There are a number of ways to finish the bottom edge of streamers. You can simply hem as you do the long edges. See figure 4. Figure 5 shows an attractive finish which can be done while hemming sides. Hem one side, fold over end and catch in other side. A third method is done after the sides are hemmed. Fold right sides together lining up side hems and simply stitch across end. Fold to outside to form point. See figure 6.

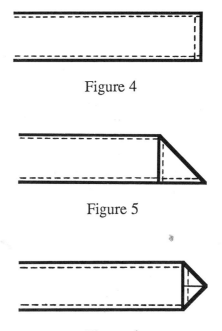

Figure 4

Figure 5

Figure 6

If you plan to make several windsocks you may want to invest in a hot knife found at hobby shops. These work by cutting and slightly melting the nylon to prevent fraying, thus eliminating the hemming. Yet another method is to trace the desired shape onto the fabric with Fray Check™ (make a durable pattern from cardboard for tracing several pieces), allow to dry and then carefully trim within the Fray Check™ line. Remember to adjust the width of streamers if you use one of these methods because all measurements in this book include hem allowances. These methods (hot knife or Fray Check™) work especially well on irregularly shaped pieces such as the streamers of the Parrot windsock or the scales of the Fish.

To attach streamers to windsock arrange them in desired order, place right sides of streamers to right side of windsock and stitch seam. If your streamers do not fit exactly along the width of the windsock do not worry about overlapping them a little. Spaces between streamers are unsightly so if you come out short it is best to add one more streamer. See figure 7.

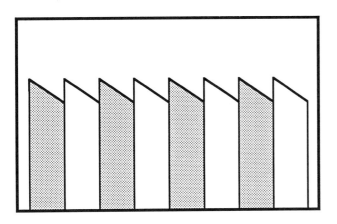

Figure 7

Unless otherwise instructed all seam allowances are 1/4" (6mm). Stitch all seams with right sides together.

You will need to finish seams inside your windsock because the nylon frays badly. If you have an overlock machine it works beautifully but zigzag or Fray Check™ work, too. Remember to secure threads to make your windsock durable because if hung outdoors it will, of course, take quite a beating. The sun is your windsock's worst enemy. To prolong the life of your creation find a place in the shade to prevent rapid fading.

## Finishing

Plastic tubing works well for hoops. You can purchase rings at hobby shops made of wood, metal or plastic but there are two disadvantages to these. First, they are much heavier than tubing, therefore, requiring more wind to move them. Secondly, these rings come in predetermined sizes. The plastic tubing can be cut to fit your creation. Polyester boning is sold in fabric stores ($1.20 per yard) and is a very stiff material used for stays in clothing and can also be used for the hoops in windsocks. The 1/2" width works well and can be inserted by simply folding the top of the windsock down over the boning and sewing in place. This flat boning gives a slightly different look to the finished product than the round tubing.

You will need to make a trip to your local hardware store for tubing. It comes in different sizes, 1/8" to 1/4" diameter works well. Be sure to get tubing that is stiff enough to hold its shape when formed into a circle. Also, at the hardware store buy a wooden dowel that fits snugly inside the tubing. Cut the dowel into 3/4" lengths to insert into both ends of tubing to form circular shape. See figure 8.

Figure 8

You will also need a fishing swivel to hang your windsock. These, too, can be found at the hardware store or sporting goods store. See figure 9. Swivels prevent strings from twisting and tangling in the wind. For a large windsock with heavy string the large swivels (number 3) work best. Nylon string works well because it is durable and can be melted at the final knot to ensure a good fasten. Hobby and craft stores carry colored string, too, which is fun to use but not as durable.

Figure 9

Turn top 1" of windsock to inside and press. Turn raw edge under 1/4" and stitch close to folded edge to form casing. Leave 3/4" to 1" opening to insert tubing. To determine length of tubing measure distance across flattened windsock and multiply by two. See figure 10. Thread the tubing (with dowel inserted in one end) through the casing and connect to other end inside the casing. Stitch opening closed. It can be difficult to get the hoop under the presser foot of your machine to close off the casing. You can remove the presser foot, insert the windsock, replace foot and close or you may simply omit this step and leave that little opening. Be sure to put one of the hanging strings in that spot to secure it.

Figure 10

You are now ready to apply strings. If you have a grommet tool you may want to use grommets in the windsock for a neater appearance but grommets or eyelets are not necessary. Cut three 24" lengths of string, fold in half and use to thread a large darning needle. At this point measure the outside circumference of your windsock at the hoop and divide by three to space strings evenly. Remember, the outside circumference is not the same as the length of the tubing. It is not as easy to "eye ball" this as you may think, so take time to measure. Attach strings by pulling ends through loop to form a simple Lark's Head knot as shown. See figure 11. This produces double cords for durability. At about 4"-6" (depending on the size of the windsock) knot all six strings together. Thread swivel onto three strands and tie second knot 3"-4" above the first. See figure 12. If using nylon trim strings close to knot

and melt over flame to secure ends. If you are not using nylon string leave adequate length so knot does not come undone.

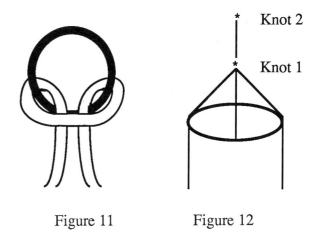

Figure 11          Figure 12

You are now ready to hang your beautiful windsock either indoors or outdoors and enjoy it!

# Children's Designs
## Animals
Approximate Length 53"

If you know a child who loves animals you may want to make this animal windsock which is divided into dinosaurs, circus animals and farm animals. Of course, you can make a windsock with only dinosaurs, circus animals or domestic animals in sections as this one or one section with long streamers. Maybe two sections? Be creative and have fun.

● You will need:

| | |
|---|---|
| 1/3 yard red | 1/4 yard green |
| 1/3 yard blue | 1/4 yard orange |
| 1/3 yard yellow | 3/4 yard Wonder Under™ |
| 1/4 yard purple | Matching Thread |

● Cut:

| | |
|---|---|
| 1 red, 18 1/2" by 11 1/2" | 3 purple bands, 3" by 18 1/2" |
| 1 blue, 18 1/2" by 11 1/2" | 8 multi colored streamers, |
| 1 yellow, 18 1/2" by 11 1/2" | 3 1/2" by 10" each |
| 1 purple band, 4" by 18 1/2" | |

Cut animal shapes from desired colors after tracing on fusible. You may use the colors suggested on each pattern piece or you may choose different color groupings.

● Method:

Fuse all animals randomly onto the three sections of the windsock. Attach all sections with purple bands between and widest purple band at top. See figure 1. Finish all seams.

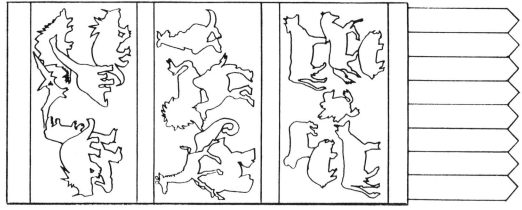

Figure 1

Hem long edges and ends of all streamers and attach to windsock as directed on page 4. Stitch, finish and press long side seam. Now turn to page 5 for finishing instructions.

Actual Size
Trace All Pieces Onto Fusible

Purple

Green

8-

Yellow

Actual Size

Trace All Pieces Onto Fusible

Red

9-

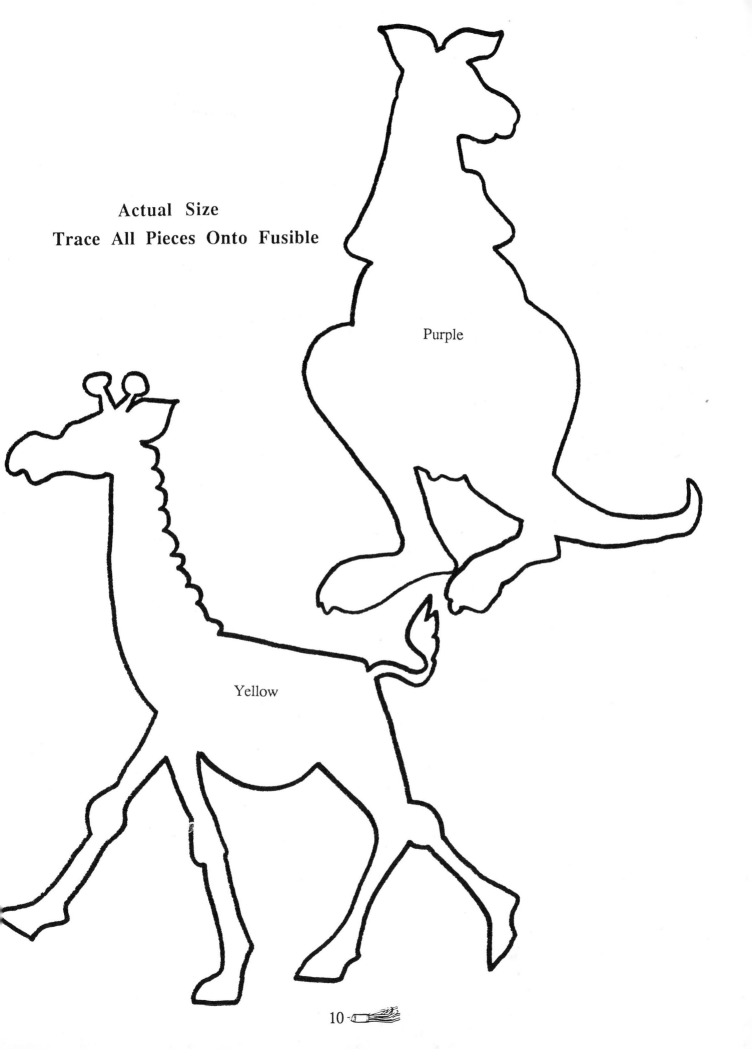

Actual Size
Trace All Pieces Onto Fusible

Purple

Yellow

10

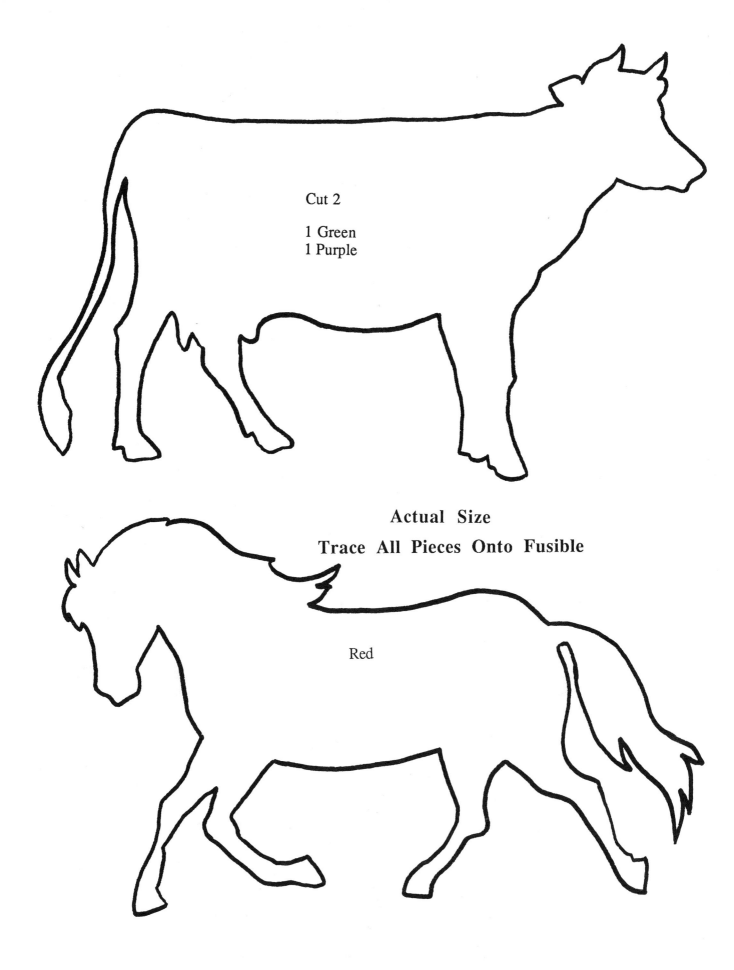

Cut 2

1 Green
1 Purple

**Actual Size**

**Trace All Pieces Onto Fusible**

Red

11

Cut 2

Blue

Orange

Orange

**Actual Size**

**Trace All Pieces Onto Fusible**

12

Green

Actual Size

Trace All Pieces Onto Fusible

Blue

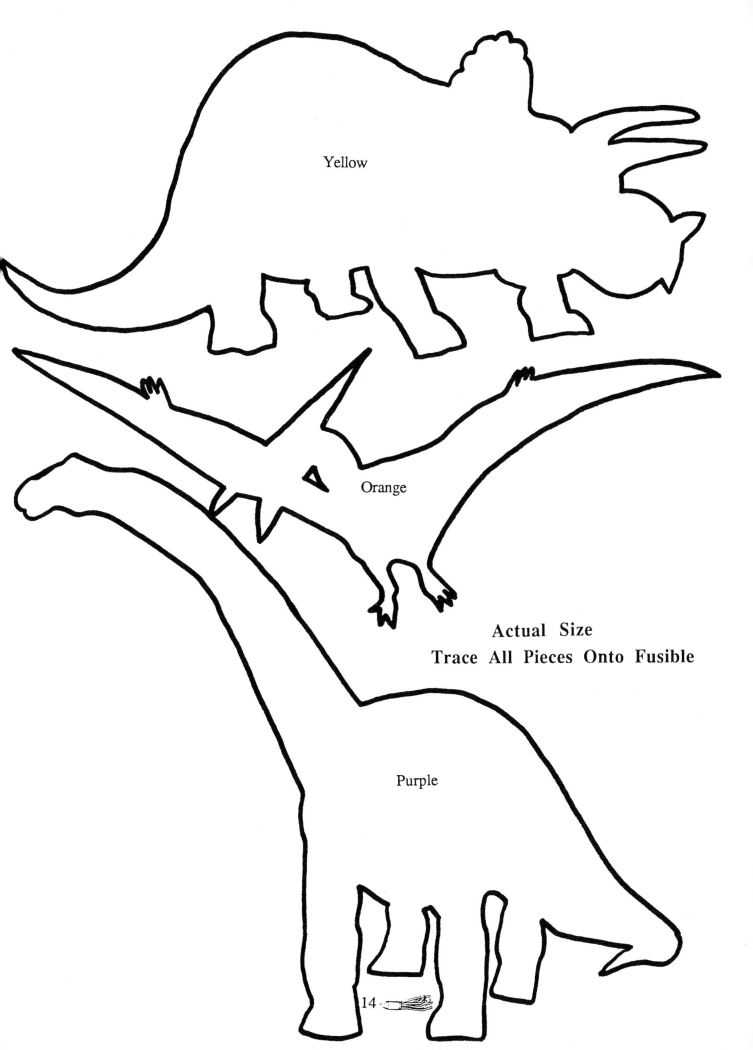

Yellow

Orange

Purple

**Actual Size**
**Trace All Pieces Onto Fusible**

14 -

# Miscellaneous Designs
## Apple
Approximate Length 58"

How about an apple windsock for your favorite teacher?  This windsock would be great for a classroom or any room.

● You will need:

> 2/3 yard tan
> 2/3 yard red
> Scraps of dark brown and green
> 1/2 yard Wonder Under™
> Matching thread

● Cut:

> 1 tan background, 9" by 21 1/2"
> 1 red band, 4 1/2" by 21 1/2"
> 1 red band, 3 1/2" by 21 1/2"
> 4 red streamers, 3 1/2" by 45"
> 4 tan streamers, 3 1/2" by 45"
> On fusible:
>> 4 red apples
>> 4 tan inside apples
>> 4 green leaves
>> 12 brown seeds
>> 4 brown stems

● Method:

Fuse red apple pieces onto background fabric spacing 1/2" apart.  Remember to allow an additional 1/4" seam allowance on sides.  Place apples on an imaginary line 2 1/4" from lower edge.  Now fuse tan "core" to left half of each apple.  Fuse stems, seeds and leaves as shown in figure 1.

Figure 1

With right sides together stitch widest red band to top edge of background piece and narrower band to lower edge. Finish seams and press. Hem 3 edges of streamers and attach to windsock as instructed on page 4. Fold windsock to inside and stitch side seam, apply seam finish and press. Page 5 gives instructions for finishing techniques.

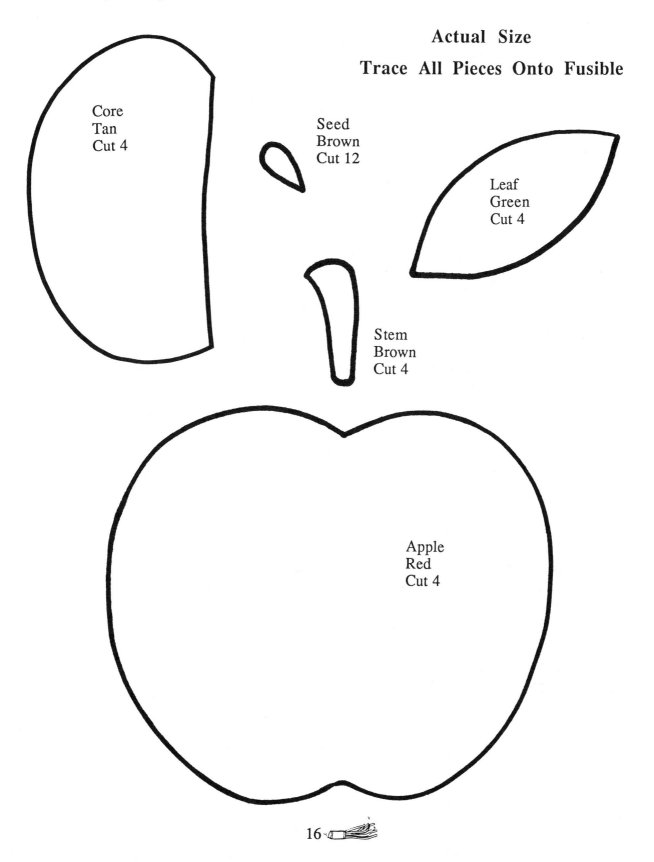

**Actual Size**

**Trace All Pieces Onto Fusible**

Core
Tan
Cut 4

Seed
Brown
Cut 12

Leaf
Green
Cut 4

Stem
Brown
Cut 4

Apple
Red
Cut 4

## Miscellaneous Designs
## Little Red Barn
Approximate Length 46"

If the decor is "Country" this windsock will fit right in.

- You will need:

  1/4 yard gray
  5/8 yard navy blue
  5/8 yard red
  1/4 yard Wonder Under™
  Matching thread

- Cut:

  1 gray background piece, 7 1/2" by 20 1/2"
  1 navy band, 2" by 20 1/2"
  1 red band, 3" by 20 1/2"
  1 red strip, 3" by 24"
  1 navy strip, 3" by 24"
  4 red streamers, 3 1/2" by 32"
  4 navy streamers, 3 1/2" by 32"
  On fusible:
  Barn pattern pieces as shown

- Method:

Fuse barn to center of gray background piece. You may want to use a machine satin stitch to add barn doors for more detail. (See page 3.)

Stitch red and navy 24" strips together as shown in figure 1. Finish seam and press.

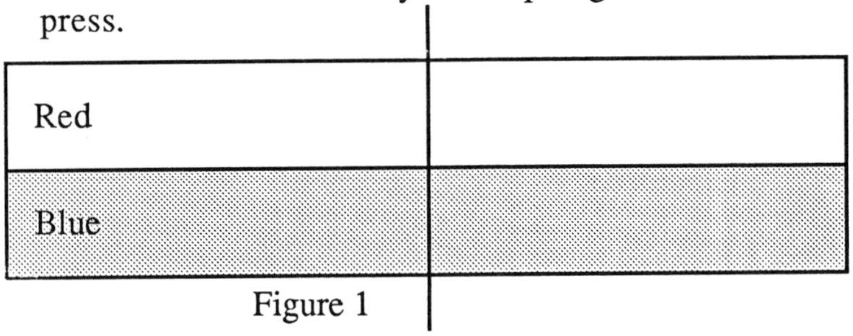
Red
Blue

Cut at center as shown.

Figure 1

Stitch these 2 sections together as shown in figure 2. Finish seam and press.

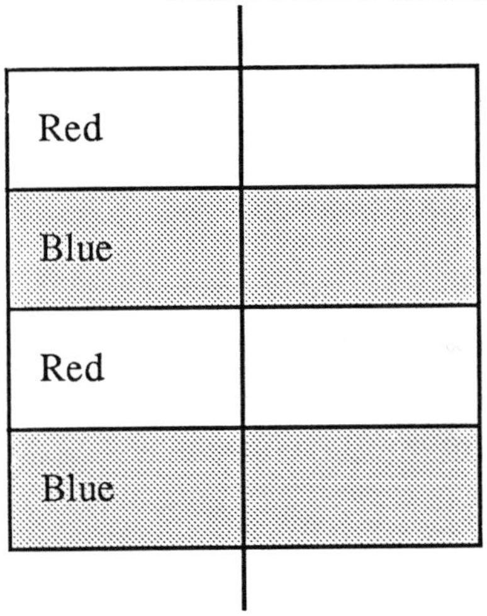
Red
Blue
Red
Blue

Figure 2

Cut at center again as shown.

Repeat this process one more time to create 2 checked bands. (Figure 3)

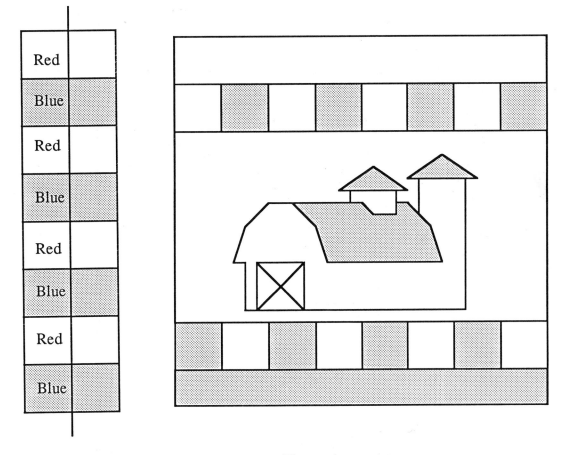

|  |  |
|---|---|
| Red | |
| Blue | |
| Red | |
| Blue | |
| Red | |
| Blue | |
| Red | |
| Blue | |

Figure 3                    Figure 4

Apply 1 checked band and red band to top edge and 1 checked band and blue band to lower edge of gray piece as shown in figure 4. Finish seams and press. Hem long edges and ends of all streamers and attach to windsock as directed on page 4. Stitch final side seam, finish and press. You are now ready to turn to page 5 to complete your Little Red Barn windsock.

Actual Size

Trace All Pieces Onto Fusible

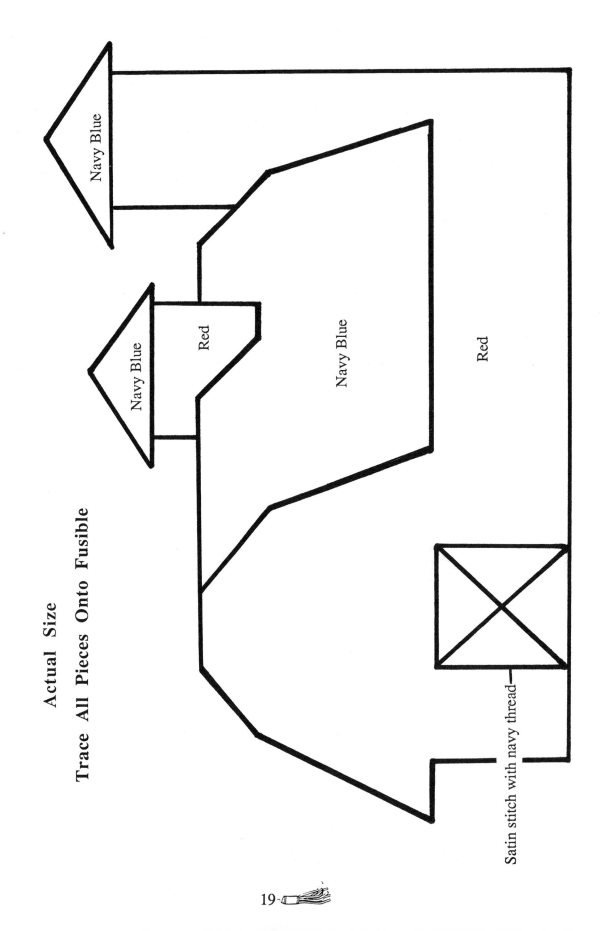

Navy Blue

Navy Blue

Red

Navy Blue

Red

Satin stitch with navy thread

## Miscellaneous Designs
## Birthday Cake
Approximate Length 55"

What a fun way to add to the birthday celebration for those special people at your house.  Or as a gift for your friends this "birthday cake" is certainly fun and unique.

● You will need:

| | |
|---|---|
| 1/3 yard white | 1/8 yard orange |
| 1/8 yard gray | 1/8 yard red |
| 1/3 yard blue | 1/2 yard Wonder Under™ |
| 1/3 yard hot pink | Matching thread |
| 1/8 yard purple | |
| 1/8 yard green | |
| 1/8 yard yellow | |

● Cut:

1 white background, 10 1/2" by 22"
1 gray band, 3 1/2" by 22"
9 streamers of various colors, 3 1/2" by 44"
On fusible:
    2" blue letters spelling "HAPPY BIRTHDAY"
    2 pink "icing" scallops, 22" each
    5 pink "icing" flowers
    5 pink "icing" sashes
    10 multi colored candles
    10 flames, yellow and orange as shown

● Method:

Fuse candles and flames to white background as shown in figure 1.  Space candles approximately 1 1/2" apart and in line 4" from lower edge.  Fuse "HAPPY BIRTHDAY" to gray band remembering to allow for 1/4" seam allowances.  With right sides together stitch gray band to lower edge of "cake".  Finish seam and press.

Figure 1

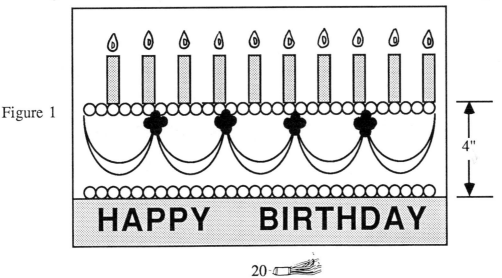

Figure 1 also shows scalloped icing fused over base of candles and directly over seam line.  Now space sashes between rows of "icing" and fuse into place.  Fuse 4 flowers as shown.  Hem long edges and lower ends of all streamers and turn to page 4 for instructions for attaching them to windsock.  Stitch side seam, finish seam and press.  Placing a pressing ham inside windsock fuse final flower directly over seam line for a symmetrical design.

Turn to page 5 for final directions for adding a hoop and strings to your Birthday Cake windsock.

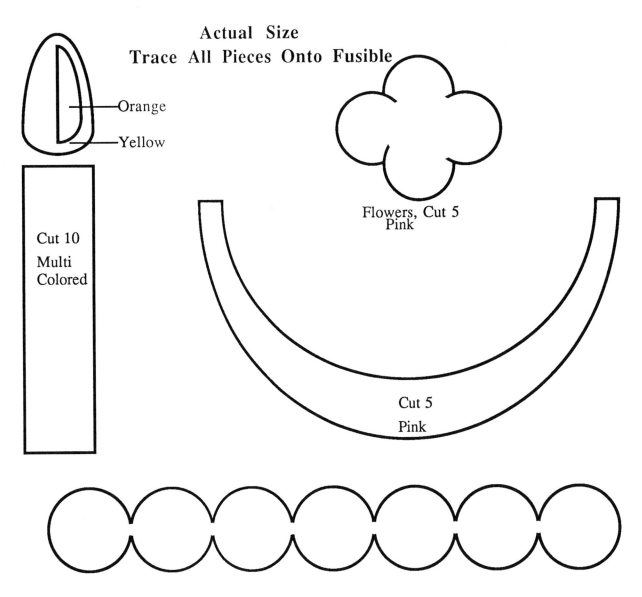

**Actual Size**
**Trace All Pieces Onto Fusible**

Orange

Yellow

Cut 10
Multi
Colored

Flowers, Cut 5
Pink

Cut 5

Pink

Cut 2 Pink Scalloped Bands, Each 22"

# Miscellaneous Designs
## Business Logo
### Approximate Length 27"

Most any business logo can be worked into a windsock. This particular one (Central Minnesota Divers) is quite detailed and was screen printed onto rip stop nylon for a quick windsock and instant advertising. Of course, many simple logos can be traced onto a fusible, cut out of nylon and applied.

● You will need:

        1/3 yard blue
        1/3 yard white
        1/4 yard Wonder Under™
        Matching thread

● Cut:

        1 white background, 5" by 18"
        4 white bands, 1 1/2" by 18"
        5 blue bands, 1 1/2" by 18
        1 blue band, 2 1/2" by 18"
        3 blue streamers, 4" by 15"
        3 white streamers, 4" by 15"
        Your logo on fusible

● Method:

Fuse logo to background piece centering appropriately for your design. Stitch all bands to this center piece alternating colors. Be sure widest blue band is at top edge for casing. Finish seams and press. Hem long edges and ends of all streamers and apply to windsock as directed on page 4. Stitch side seam, finish, press and turn to page 5 for finishing techniques.

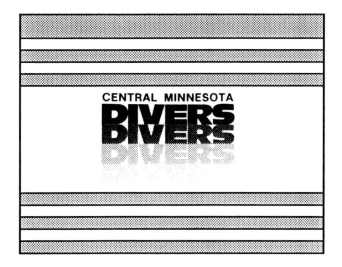

## Miscellaneous Designs
## Cal Poly
### Approximate Length 50"

This windsock would make a great gift for the college student. Or perhaps your group would like to make and sell them as a fundraiser? Whatever the reason everyone loves their Alma Mater and with a bit of designing you can create individualized windsocks. Of course, you will want to use appropriate school colors. Next you will need to find a map of your state and trace its shape (enlarge or decrease size if necessary). Turn to the alphabet letters at the end of this book and trace those you need. Now follow these simple directions.

● You will need:              ● Cut:

    1/2 yard yellow              1 yellow background, 10 1/2" by 18"
    1/2 yard green              1 green band, 4 1/2" by 18"
    1/8 yard white              1 green band, 3 1/2" by 18"
    1/2 yard Wonder Under™     1 white "state" on fusible
    Matching thread            1 green star on fusible
                             Green letters to spell name of university on fusible
                             4 green streamers, 3 1/2" by 34"
                             4 yellow streamers, 3 1/2" by 34"

● Method:

Fuse state and name of university to background piece. Mark location of your town and school with a star as shown. With right sides together attach widest green band to top and narrow band to lower edge. Finish seams and press. See figure 1.

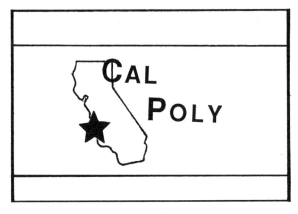

Figure 1

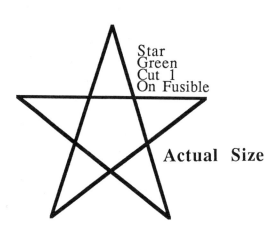

Star
Green
Cut 1
On Fusible

**Actual Size**

Cal Poly is at San Luis Obispo, California. Make this windsock your very own by substituting your state, town and school.

Hem long edges and lower edge of each streamer and attach to windsock as directed on page 4. On page 5 you will find finishing instructions.

## Miscellaneous Designs
## Checkerboard
Approximate Length 48"

This Checkerboard windsock is not nearly as time consuming to make as you may think. Follow the tricks below and you will see that this windsock can be a fun and successful project even for the beginner.

● You will need:

    1/2 yard light pink
    1/2 yard burgundy
    1/4 yard Wonder Under™
    Matching thread

● Cut:

Light Pink:
    1 rectangle, 6" by 20"
    2 strips, 2 1/2" by 25"
    1 streamer piece, 12" by 27"
    3 strips, 2 1/2" by 12"

Burgundy:
    1 top band, 3" by 20"
    2 strips, 2 1/2" by 25"
    1 streamer piece, 12" by 27"
    3 strips, 2 1/2" by 12"
    6 flower designs on fusible

● Method:

Fuse five flower designs to pink piece as shown in figure 1. After the side seam is stitched the sixth flower is fused over the seam line for a symmetrical design. This can be done with a pressing ham inside the windsock or by placing the windsock over the end of your ironing board.

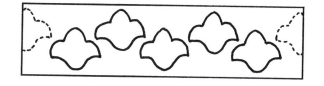

Figure 1.

Figure 2 shows the two light strips (2 1/2" by 25") and the same size two dark strips stitched together in an alternating pattern. Cut this piece into 2 1/2" strips as indicated in figure 2. Figure 3 shows design after offsetting strips to create checkerboard effect. Do this by "flipping" every other strip end for end. Do not just "shift" strips or you will end up with a piece that looks like figure 4 with only three usable rows of blocks.

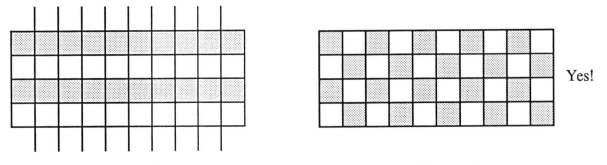

Figure 2                                    Figure 3

Yes!

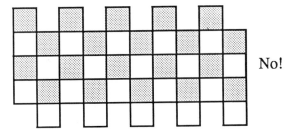

No!

Figure 4

Stitch 2 1/2" strips to end of streamer piece as is shown in figure 5. On light piece alternate strips dark, light, dark and reverse the order on the dark streamer piece. Finish seams. Cut each of these pieces lengthwise into three 4" strips as indicated. Hem all six streamers on long edges and lower edges.

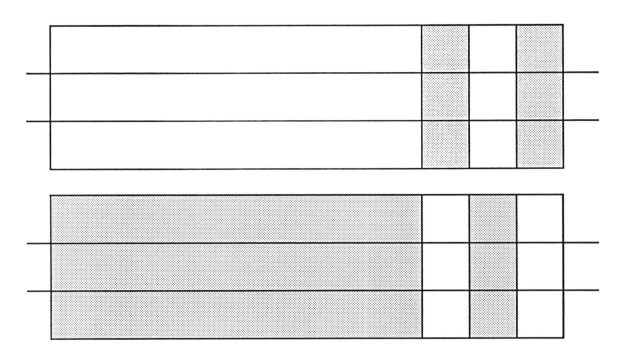

Figure 5

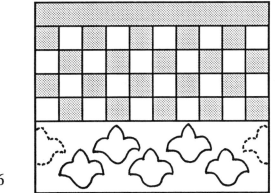

Figure 6

With right sides together stitch flower design piece to lower edge of checked piece and attach top band. Finish seams. Follow directions on page 4 for attaching streamers to windsock. Fold windsock to inside to stitch side seam, finish seam and press. Now fuse final flower centered over seam line. Turn to page 5 for instructions for casing, hoop and strings to complete your windsock.

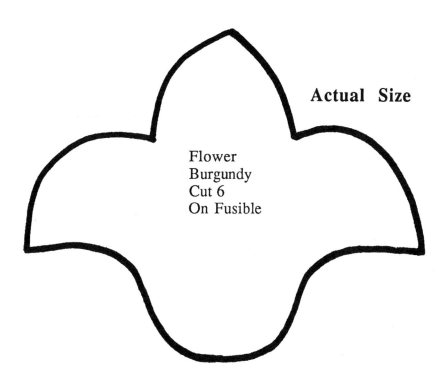

**Actual Size**

Flower
Burgundy
Cut 6
On Fusible

# Seasonal Designs
# Christmas
## Approximate Length 62"

Add to the festivities this holiday season with this Christmas windsock. Make it for yourself or as a gift. Or wouldn't this make a great bazaar item for your group to sell?

● You will need:

    2/3 yard green
    1/3 yard red
    5/8 yard white
    1/2 yard Wonder Under™
    Matching thread

● Cut:

    1 white, 10 1/2" by 21 1/2"
    2 red bands, 2" by 21 1/2"
    1 green band, 1 1/2" by 21 1/2"
    1 green band, 3" by 21 1/2"
    3 green streamers, 4" by 45"
    2 red streamers, 4" by 45"
    2 white streamers, 4" by 45"
    On fusible:
        9 green holly leaves
        9 red holly berries

● Method:

Fuse holly leaves and berries to white background as shown. Figure 1 also shows red and green bands attached to top and bottom edges. Be sure widest green band is at top edge to allow for the casing. Finish seams and press.

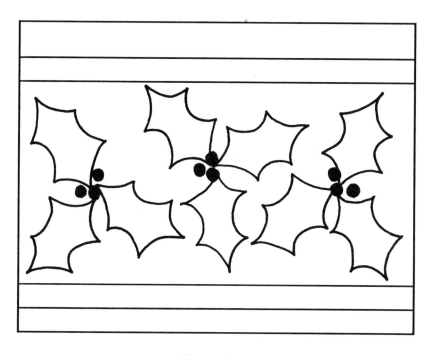

Figure 1

Hem long edges and lower edge of each streamer and attach to windsock as instructed on page 4. On page 5 are instructions for finishing your Christmas windsock.

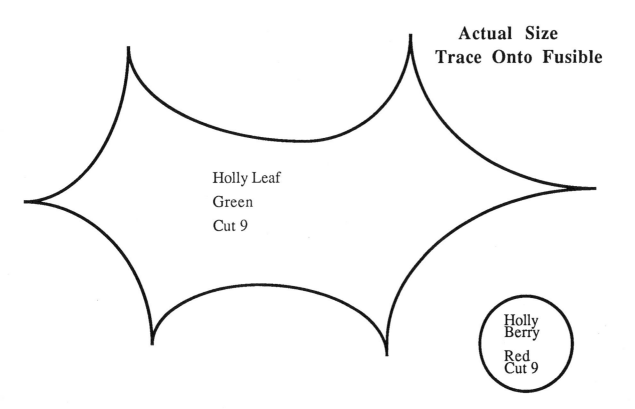

**Actual Size**
**Trace Onto Fusible**

Holly Leaf

Green

Cut 9

Holly
Berry

Red
Cut 9

## Miscellaneous Designs
## Cows
### Approximate Length 44"

For your dairy farmer friends or that person who collects cows, these Holsteins are sure to please.

● You will need:

    5/8 yard green
    1/3 yard black
    1/3 yard white
    1/2 yard Wonder Under™
    Matching thread

● Cut:

    1 green square, 19 1/2" by 19 1/2"
    3 black strips, 3" by 19 1/2"
    3 white strips, 3" by 19 1/2"
    3 green strips, 3" by 19 1/2"
    1 black strip, 4" by 19 1/2"
    5 white cows on fusible

● Method:

Trace the 5 cows onto Wonder Under™, reversing the pattern so some cows face the opposite direction. Use whichever tails you like best to add interest to your "herd". Fuse all 5 cows on white nylon and then fuse blotches of black randomly to create 5 individuals. It works best and saves time if you apply blotches before cutting out cows so outside edges need only be cut once.

Fuse cows in the arrangement you like on the green square. See figure 1. Stitch the widest black strip to the top of this piece and stitch all other strips together alternating colors. Now attach this striped piece to the "pasture", stitch long side seam, finish and press. Turn windsock right side out and by machine make a narrow rolled hem on the bottom edge. You are now ready for the casing and hoop instructions found on page 5.

Figure 1

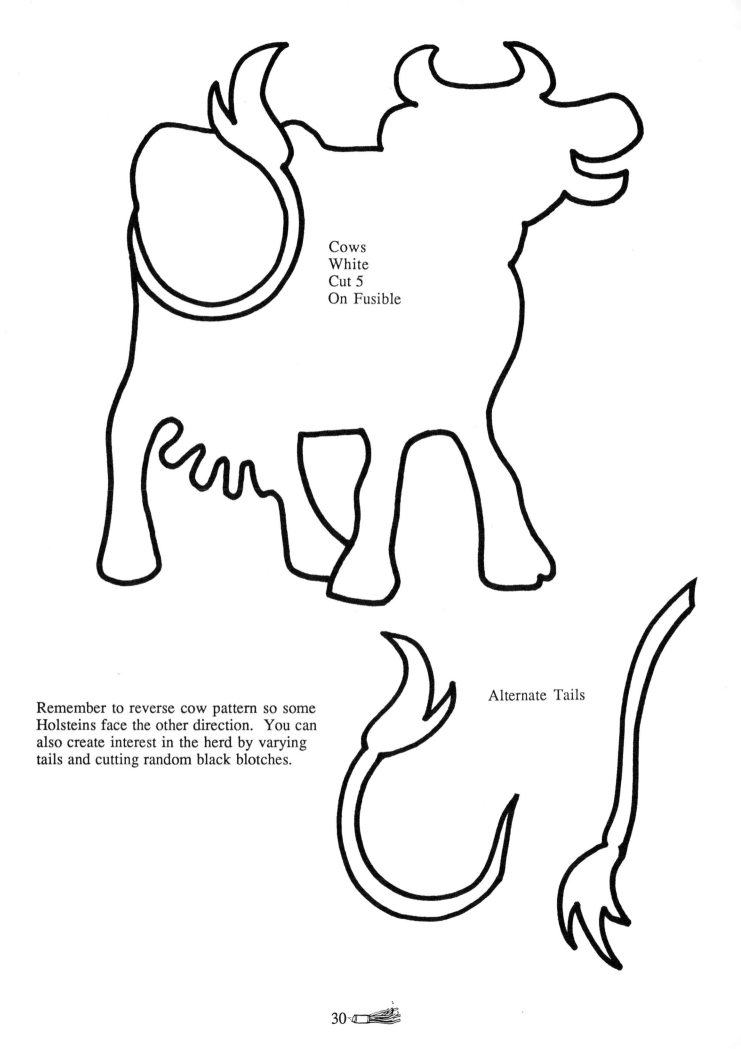

Cows
White
Cut 5
On Fusible

Alternate Tails

Remember to reverse cow pattern so some
Holsteins face the other direction. You can
also create interest in the herd by varying
tails and cutting random black blotches.

# Seasonal Designs
## Easter Lilies
### Approximate Length 45"

Easter Lilies are such a welcome sign of spring and new life. Even if you do not have a "green thumb" you can show off these lilies.

● You will need:

> 1/4 yard dark purple
> 1/2 yard lavender
> 1/2 yard white
> Scraps of yellow
> 1/2 yard Wonder Under™
> Matching thread

● Cut:

> 1 dark purple, 8" by 18"
> 1 lavender band, 2 1/2" by 18"
> 1 lavender band, 3 1/2" by 18"
> 4 lavender streamers, 3 1/2" by 33"
> 3 white streamers, 3 1/2" by 33"
> 2 white of each lily pattern on fusible
> 4 yellow flower centers on fusible

● Method:

Fuse lilies onto purple background piece in random pattern, adding more flowers if you prefer. Fuse little yellow centers to flowers where appropriate. Attach widest lavender band to top edge and narrow band to lower edge as shown in figure 1.

Figure 1

Hem long edges and ends of all streamers and attach to windsock as shown on page 4. Stitch side seam, finish and press. Turn to page 5 for finishing instructions.

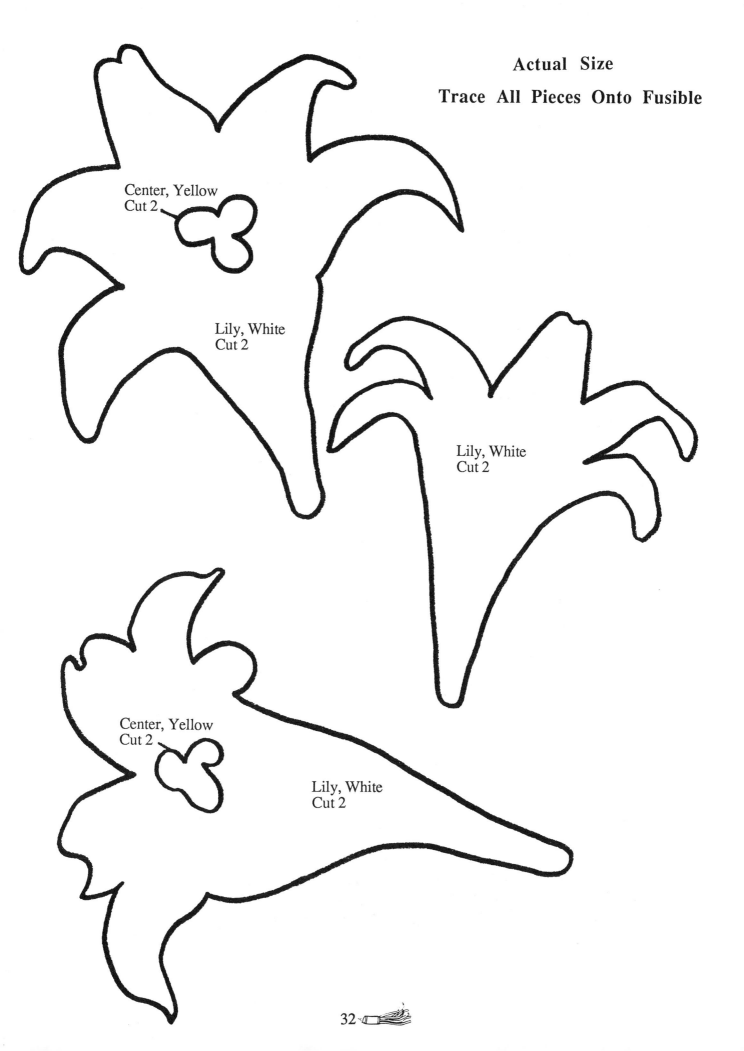

Actual Size

Trace All Pieces Onto Fusible

Center, Yellow
Cut 2

Lily, White
Cut 2

Lily, White
Cut 2

Center, Yellow
Cut 2

Lily, White
Cut 2

## Miscellaneous Designs
## Fish
### Approximate Length 42"

No windsock pattern book would be complete without the traditional fish design. You will want to use a hot knife or Fray Check™ to finish edges of the fins, scales and tail. Directions for this are found on page 4.

● You will need:

  2/3 yard black
  1/2 yard turquoise
  1/3 yard purple
  1/3 yard hot pink
  Scraps of white
  Scraps of Wonder Under™
  Black thread

● Cut:

  All enlarged pattern pieces as shown, finishing edges as directed
  On fusible:
    2 white circles
    2 black circles

● Method:

Layer scalloped scales alternating colors as desired. Begin at lower end of windsock, stitch first scales close to edge as shown in figure 1.

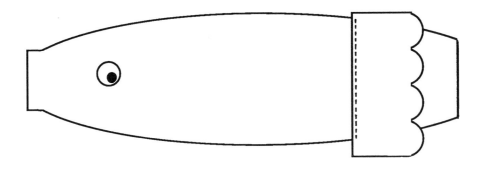

Figure 1

Repeat with next 4 rows spacing each one 3"-4" above last. Final row must be attached right sides together as shown in figure 2. Stitch seam, fold down and press. From wrong side trim all scales to fit fish shape. Baste edges.

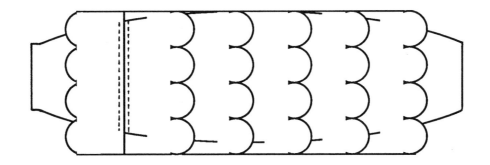

Figure 2

With right sides together stitch tail pieces at lower edges of fish front and back sections. Finish seams and press. Fuse black dot to larger white dot to make eye and fuse to fish as shown on pattern.

Baste fins to sides of fish and with right sides together stitch 2 long side seams being careful to catch fins in seam. Do not stitch onto tail section since these edges are finished and tail remains open.

Finish top opening as directed on page 6. Because the opening of this windsock is small only 2 strings are needed for hanging.

Eye, Actual Size

Cut 2 White and 2 Black on Fusible

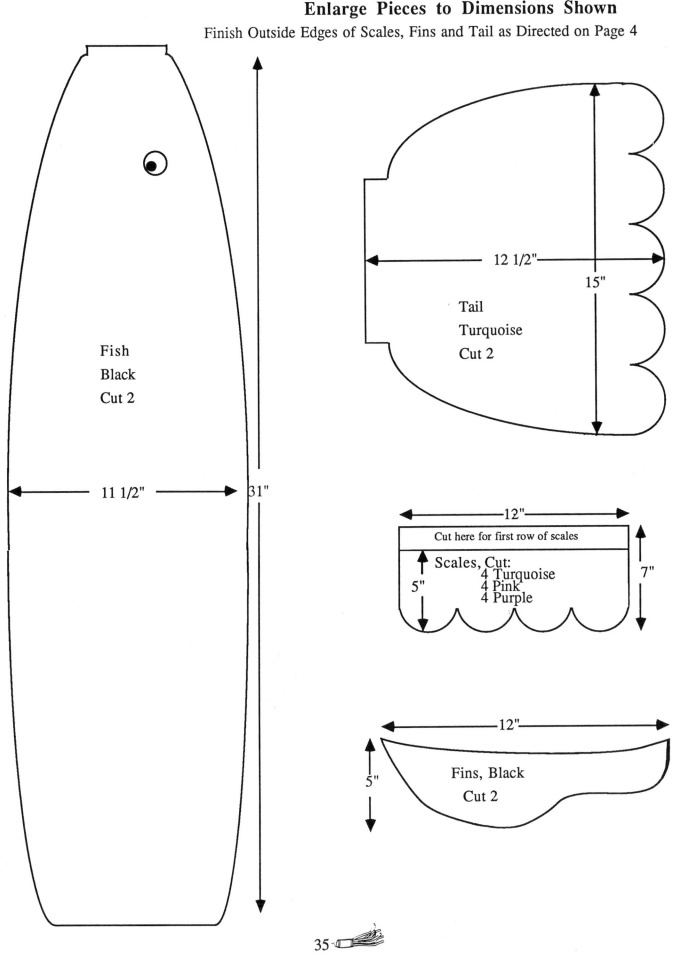

**Enlarge Pieces to Dimensions Shown**
Finish Outside Edges of Scales, Fins and Tail as Directed on Page 4

Fish
Black
Cut 2

11 1/2"

31"

Tail
Turquoise
Cut 2

12 1/2"

15"

12"

Cut here for first row of scales

Scales, Cut:
4 Turquoise
4 Pink
4 Purple

5"

7"

12"

Fins, Black
Cut 2

5"

## Miscellaneous Designs
## It's A Boy!
### Approximate Length 54"

What a fun way to announce this important news! You may want to make several of these windsocks to have on hand as gifts. Of course, use shades of pink and change lettering to "It's A Girl!" or how about "We Have Twins!"

● You will need:

     5/8 yard white
     1/2 yard dark blue
     1/2 yard light blue
     1/8 yard Wonder Under™
     Matching thread

● Cut:

     1 white background, 6 1/2" by 24"
     3 light blue strips, 3" by 20"
     2 dark blue strips, 3" by 20"
     1 white band, 4" by 32"
     1 white band, 3" by 32"
     2 white streamers, 4" by 40"
     2 light blue streamers, 4" by 40"
     3 dark blue streamers, 4" by 40"
     2" letters traced on fusible  (find at end of book)

● Method:

In order to create a diagonal design you must offset each strip as you sew them together. (Figure 1).  Stitch seams, finish and press.  Draw cutting line across long edges  and trim off corners as shown.

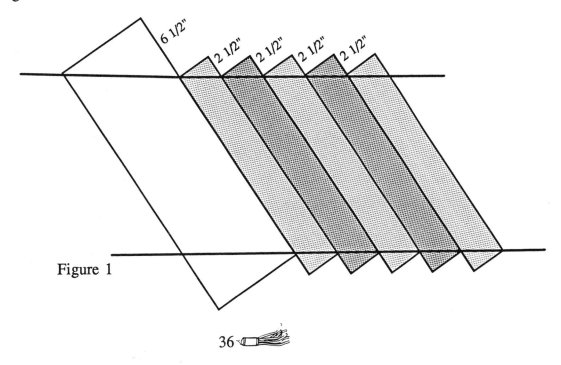

Figure 1

Stitch the 4" by 32" white band across the top edge of the windsock and the 3" by 32" band on the lower edge. Finish seams and press. Trim corners to correct angles as shown in figure 2.

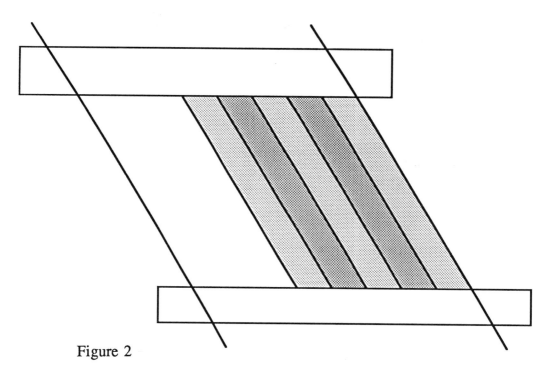

Figure 2

Fuse the message on at this point. It is easy to misjudge the letter placement if you apply the message before creating the diagonal design. Hem all long edges and ends of each streamer and attach to windsock as instructed on page 4. Fold windsock to inside and stitch the diagonal side seam, finish and press. Turn to page 5 for final instructions.

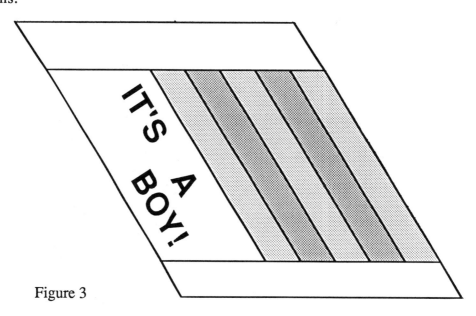

Figure 3

# Seasonal Designs
## Jack-O-Lantern
Approximate Length 46"

Welcome little spooks and goblins next Halloween with this Jack-O-Lantern windsock. There is some piecing involved but even the beginner can make this Halloween decoration.

● You will need:

        1/2 yard orange
        1/3 yard black
        1/3 yard green  (you will need this much to cut a bias strip)
        1/4 yard Wonder Under™
        1 2/3 yard 1/2" polyester boning
        Matching thread

● Cut:

        6 orange convex pattern pieces as shown
        3 green leaves with edges finished  (see instructions below)
        1 green bias strip 3" by 13", see figure 1

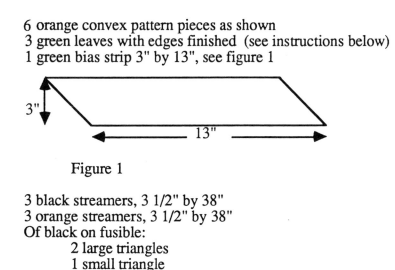

Figure 1

3 black streamers, 3 1/2" by 38"
3 orange streamers, 3 1/2" by 38"
Of black on fusible:
        2 large triangles
        1 small triangle
        1 "smile"

● Method:

Fuse face onto one of orange sections remembering to allow 1/4" seam allowances on sides as shown in figure 2. With right sides together stitch all 6 orange pieces at side seams to form spherical shape. Finish seams. Hem long edges and ends of all streamers. With right sides together, alternating colors, space them within lower opening of Jack-O-Lantern and stitch into place. Finish seam.

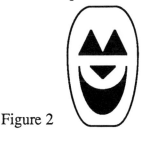

Figure 2

There are various ways to make the leaves.  You can cut them with a hot knife, trace with Fray Check™ and cut or you can use the instructions for machine applique on page 3.   To do this use a narrow satin stitch and stitch around leaf shapes  traced onto nylon.  You will want to work with two layers of nylon for stability and use a tear away stabilizer as well.  After stitching apply Fray Check™ right over stitching and allow to dry.  Carefully trim very close to stitching.  You may also want to add a line of satin stitching down the center of each leaf for added interest.

Tack  leaves to top of Jack-O-Lantern spacing them as you like.  See figure 3.

Figure 3

Stitch ends of green bias strip together to form circle.  With right sides together attach bias strip to top of Jack-O-Lantern catching leaves.  Now cut 12 1/2" length of plastic tubing as described on page 5 and form into circle attaching with 3/4" length of dowel.  Fold green bias piece over this hoop and "stitch in the ditch" from the right side catching green which is tucked to the inside.  Since this is a bias strip no seam allowance is necessary.  See figure 4.

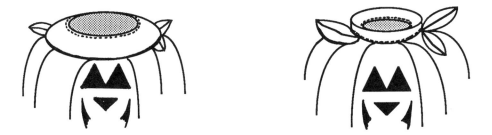

Figure 4

In order to insure a round shape to your Jack-O-Lantern you may want to add stays.  To do this cut 6 lengths of 1/2" polyester boning, each 10" long.  On inside tack these at both top and bottom at all 6 seam lines.  Now refer to page 5 for adding strings and finishing your wonderful Halloween windsock.

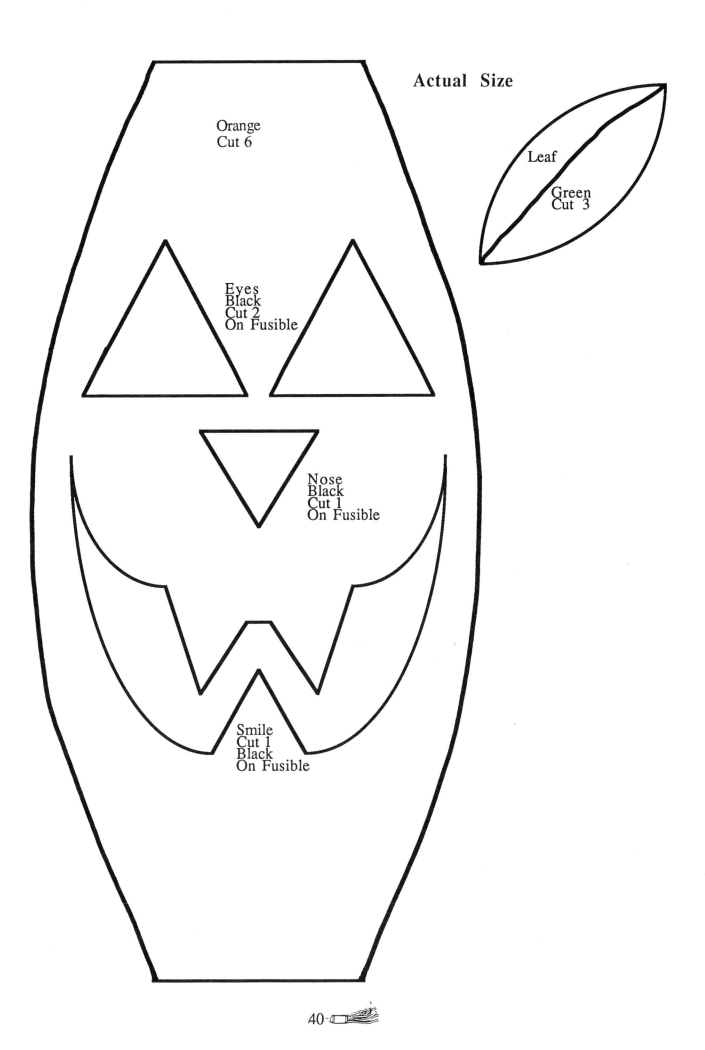

Actual Size

Orange
Cut 6

Leaf

Green
Cut 3

Eyes
Black
Cut 2
On Fusible

Nose
Black
Cut 1
On Fusible

Smile
Cut 1
Black
On Fusible

## Miscellaneous Designs
## Keyboard
Approximate Length 55"

What a fun windsock for the piano teacher to fly or maybe you would like to use it to draw attention to your music store.

● You will need:

    1/8 yard red
    3/4 yard white
    1/2 yard black
    1/4 yard Wonder Under™
    Matching thread

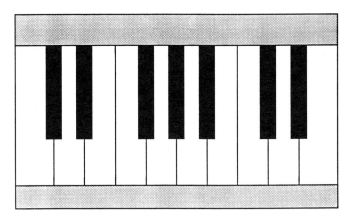

● Cut:

Figure 1

    1 white background, 11" by 20 1/2"
    7 black keys from pattern shown on fusible
    1 red band, 3 1/2" by 20 1/2" for top border
    1 red band, 2 1/2" by 20 1/2" for bottom border
    4 black streamers, 3 1/2" by 41"
    4 white streamers, 3 1/2" by 41"

● Method:

With pencil mark white rectangle into 10 equal spaces, each 2" wide (remember seam allowances on edges). This determines position for "keys". Fuse black keys in groups of 2 or 3 as shown in figure 1. You will need to make the dividing lines between white keys by machine satin stitching as described on page 3. Placing right sides together stitch widest red border on top and narrow one on lower edge. Hem 3 edges of all 8 streamers. Alternating black and white streamers, attach streamers as instructed on page 4. Follow finishing directions for casing, hoop and strings on page 5.

Piano Key

Black, Cut 7

On Fusible

**Actual Size**

## Miscellaneous  Designs
## Open
Approximate Length 50"

Let potential customers know at a glance that your store is open for business. You could work up your business logo onto this windsock and retain the "Open" words on the streamers.  Windsocks make great eye catching and inexpensive advertising.

● You will need:

3/4 yard white
1/2 yard green
1/2 yard hot pink
1/2 yard Wonder Under™
Matching thread

● Cut:

1 white background, 17" by 24 1/2"
1 green band, 3" by 24 1/2"
1 green band, 2" by 24 1/2"
3 pink streamers, 4 1/2" by 32"
2 green streamers, 4 1/2" by 32"
2 white streamers, 4 1/2" by 32"
On fusible:
9 pink "OPEN" words
8 green "OPEN" words
5 white "OPEN" words
1 pink dot
16 green dots
5 white dots

● Method:

Trace all letters (2") and dots onto Wonder Under™, fuse to appropriate colors and cut out .  Arrange pink and green words on white background as shown in figure 1.  Allow 1 inch between rows and space letters to allow 1/4" seam allowance on edges.  Fuse all letters in place with green dots between words.  With right sides together stitch  green bands to top and lower edges of background piece being careful widest band is at top.

```
OPEN ● OPEN ● OPEN ●
EN ● OPEN ● OPEN ● OP
OPEN ● OPEN ● OPEN ●
EN ● OPEN ● OPEN ● OP
OPEN ● OPEN ● OPEN ●
```

Wide Green Band
Pink, Green, Pink
Green, Pink, Green, Green
Pink, Green, Pink
Green, Pink, Green, Green
Pink, Green, Pink
Narrow Green Band

Figure 1

Fuse word "OPEN" and dot onto each streamer as shown in figure 2.

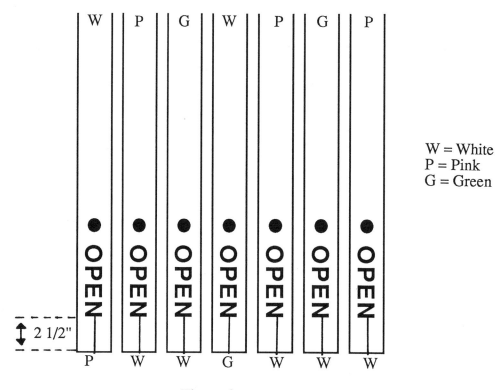

W = White
P = Pink
G = Green

Figure 2

Hem long edges and lower edge of all streamers and attach to windsock as directed on page 4.  Also, see page 5 for finishing instructions to complete and hang your advertising windsock.

Dot
Actual Size

Trace Onto Fusible:
1 Pink
5 White
16 Green

## Miscellaneous Designs
## Parrot
Approximate Length 45"

The streamers on this Parrot windsock add interest and are fun to make. You may want to use this type on other windsocks as well. They must be cut with a hot knife or traced and cut with Fray Check™ as described earlier. Also, due to the shape of the streamers you will need more fabric to make this windsock.

● You will need:

> 1/2 yard tan
> 1/4 yard light blue, dark blue, red, purple, orange, yellow, pink, peach, burgundy and gold*
> Scraps of 3 shades of green
> 1/2 yard Wonder Under™
> Dark blue thread
> Black thread

*To complete this windsock as shown in cover photo you will need 1/4 yard of all the colors listed. However, if you are careful you can cut 2 streamers from 1/4 yard so you may wish to purchase only 5 colors rather than 10. Keep in mind, however, that you will need scraps of certain colors to complete the parrot and leaves.

● Cut:

> Background piece from pattern shown
> 10 multi colored streamers from pattern shown
> 1 dark blue band, 3 1/2" by 17"
> On fusible:
> > Parrot pattern pieces as shown
> > Leaves of 3 shades of green

● Method:

Fuse parrot pieces and leaves to background as shown in figure 1.

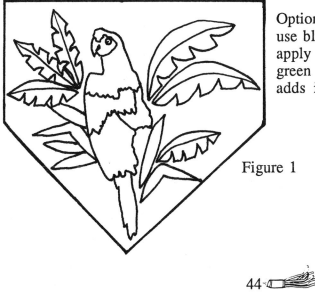

Optional: To add detail you may want to use black thread to satin stitch (page 3) to apply eye and darken inside of beak. Also, green lines stitched down center of leaves adds interest.

Figure 1

Attach blue band to top of windsock, finish seam and press. Baste 5 streamers to each side of windsock in same manner as described on page 4, arranging them so they meet at center. (Figure 2). Finish seam and press. Stitch side seam, finish and press.

Now turn to page 5 for final instructions.

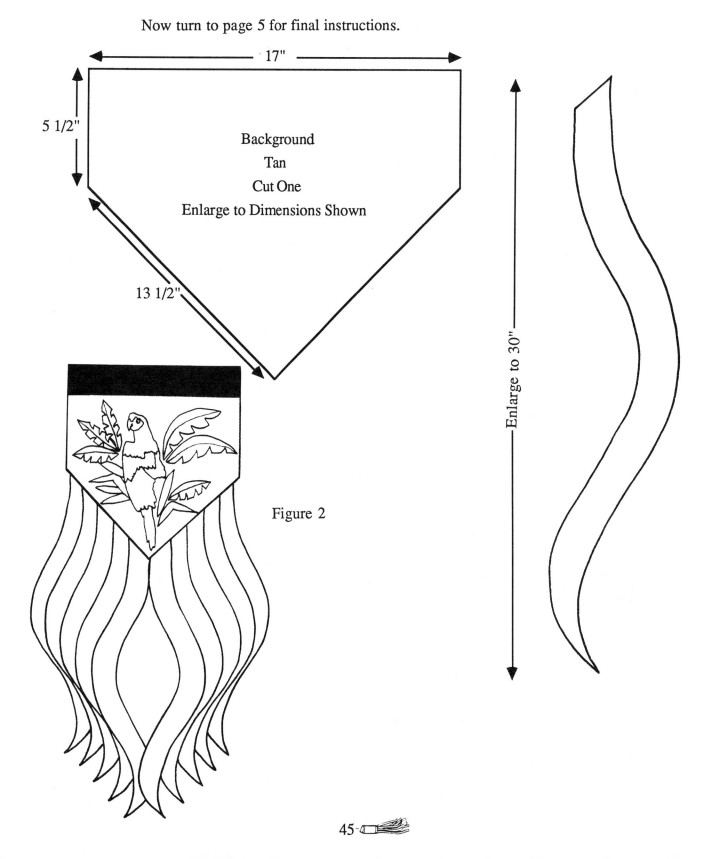

17"

5 1/2"

Background
Tan
Cut One
Enlarge to Dimensions Shown

13 1/2"

Enlarge to 30"

Figure 2

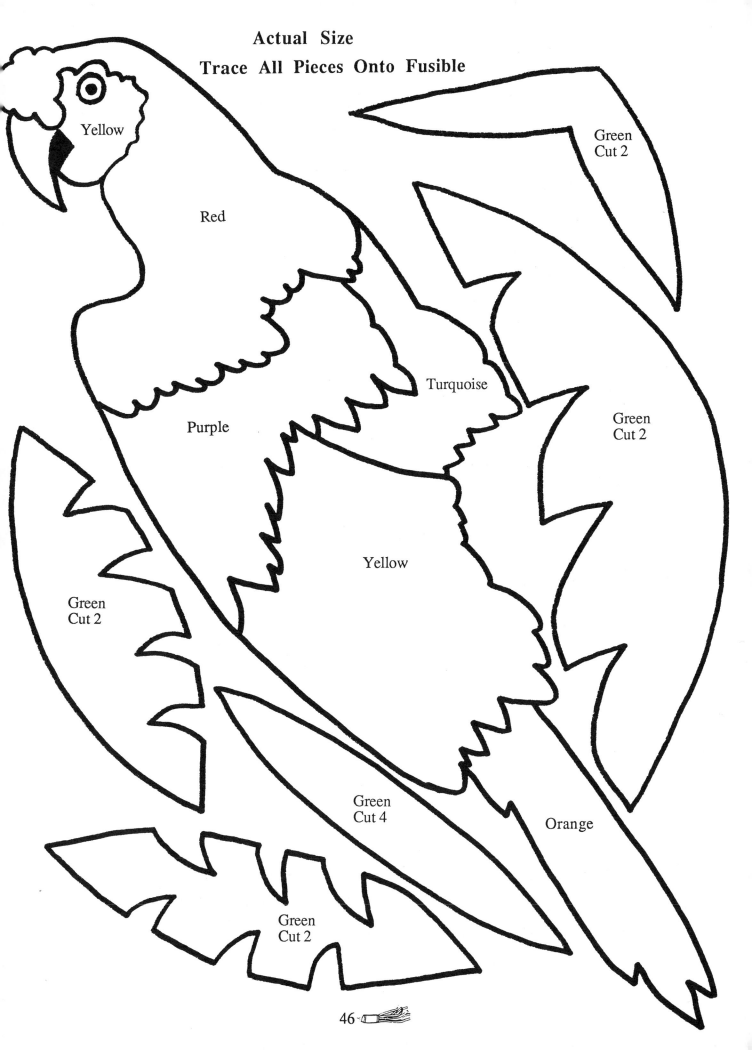

**Actual Size**
**Trace All Pieces Onto Fusible**

Yellow

Green
Cut 2

Red

Turquoise

Green
Cut 2

Purple

Green
Cut 2

Yellow

Green
Cut 2

Green
Cut 4

Orange

Green
Cut 2

46-

## Miscellaneous Designs
## Rainbow
Approximate Length  45"

The ever popular rainbow windsock is quick and easy to make, a wonderful choice for the beginner.

● You will need:

        1/8 yard red
        1/8 yard orange
        1/8 yard yellow
        1/8 yard green
        1/8 yard blue
        1/8 yard purple
        Matching thread

● Cut:

        1 streamer of each color, 4" by 27"
        1 red band, 4" by 18"
        1 band of all other colors, 3" by 18"

● Method:

With right sides together stitch all bands in rainbow order beginning with red. See figure 1.  Finish seams and press.

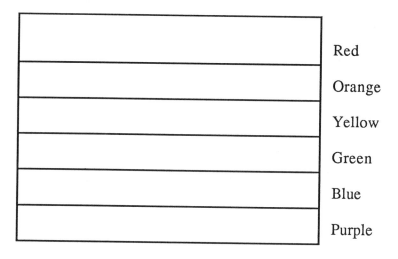

Figure 1

If you prefer a different color at the top make that color the wide one to allow for the casing.  Hem long edges and bottom edge of all streamers and attach to lower edge of windsock as directed on page 4.  Finish seam, press.  Fold windsock to inside, stitch side seam, finish and press. Turn to page 5 for finishing steps.

## Miscellaneous Designs
## Rainbow Diamond
Approximate Length 41"

Another colorful favorite is this rainbow diamond pattern. It looks much more difficult to make than it actually is so read on.

● You will need:

    1/4 yard purple
    1/4 yard blue
    1/4 yard green
    1/4 yard yellow
    1/4 yard orange
    1/4 yard red
    Matching thread

● Cut:

    6 strips (one of each color), 3" by 20"
    1 purple band, 3 1/2" by 24 1/2"
    1 red band, 2 1/2" by 24 1/2"
    6 streamers (one of each color), 4 1/2" by 30"

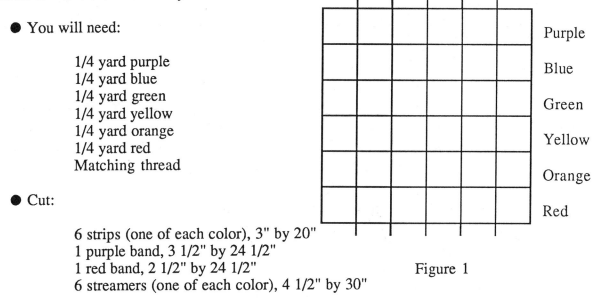

Figure 1

● Method:

Stitch all 3" strips together as shown in figure 1. Finish seams and press. Now cut this piece into 6 strips, also shown in figure 1.

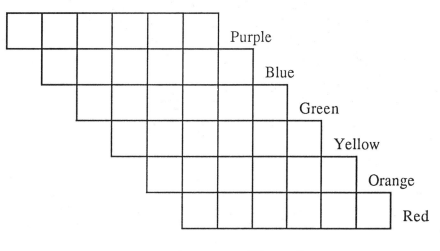

Figure 2

Figure 2 shows each new strip stitched together again after offsetting by one block.

Turn entire piece so that squares resemble diamond shapes as shown in figure 3. Draw cutting lines across long edges and trim off corners as shown allowing for 1/4" seam allowances. With right sides together stitch purple band to purple diamond edge. This will result in half purple diamonds so be sure your seam line is at the points of the blue diamonds. Repeat this step on lower edge with red band. It is easy to misjudge how far off the ends of the diamond piece these bands must extend in order to be cut at the correct angle. Therefore, pin baste and fold out to check angle before stitching this seam. Stitch, finish seams and press.

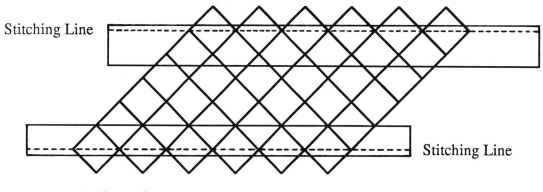

Figure 3

Trim bands to match angles. See figure 4.

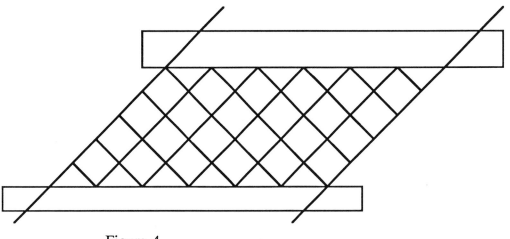

Figure 4

Hem long edges and lower ends of each streamer. Attach streamers with right sides together to red band (lower edge) of windsock as instructed on page 4. Finish seams. With right sides together stitch diagonal side seam carefully matching design.

Now turn to page 5 for final finishing directions.

# Seasonal Designs
## St. Patrick's Day
Approximate Length 45"

A "Bit 'o Green" is fun to fly for St. Patrick's Day so this windsock would make a great gift for your Irish friends. This easy to make windsock is a good project for the beginner.

● You will need:

    1/2 yard white
    1/2 yard green
    1/4 yard Wonder Under™
    Matching thread

● Cut:

    1 white background, 8" by 17"
    1 green band, 3 1/2" by 17"
    1 green band, 2 1/2" by 17"
    3 white streamers, 4" by 34"
    3 green streamers, 4" by 34"
    4 green clover leaves on fusible

● Method:

Apply the four clover leaves to background fabric in a random pattern. See figure 1. Attach wide green band to top of this piece and narrow green band to lower edge. Finish seams and press. Hem all streamers and attach as directed on page 4. Stitch side seam, finish seam and press. Turn to page 5 for finishing directions.

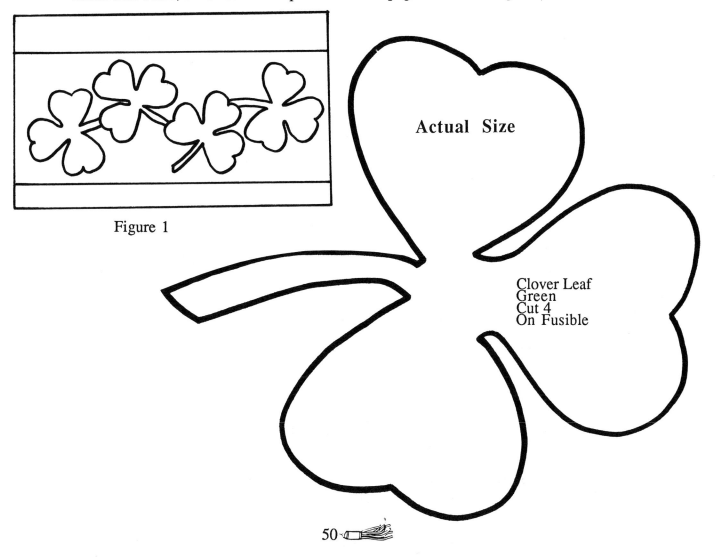

Figure 1

Actual Size

Clover Leaf
Green
Cut 4
On Fusible

# Children's Designs
## Teddy Bear
### Approximate Length 25"

This is probably the one teddy bear your collector friend still needs. With a little wind he will puff up nicely but if you wish to display him indoors just fill him with tissue paper.

● You will need:

    1 yard brown
    1/4 yard red
    1/8 yard tan
    Scraps of black and white
    1/4 yard Wonder Under™
    1/2 yard 1/2" blue ribbon
    Brown thread

● Cut:

    Body pieces from patterns shown
    1 brown bias strip, 3" by 13"

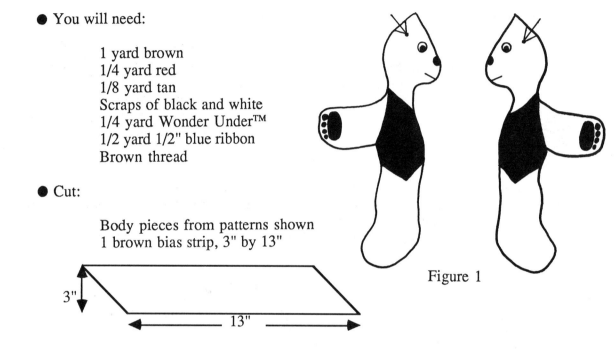

Figure 1

On fusible:
    Vest, paws, eyes, and nose from patterns shown

● Method:

Fuse vest, paws, eyes, and nose to 2 front pieces as shown in figure 1.

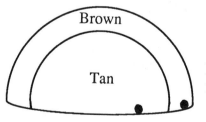

Figure 2

Figure 2 shows tan inside of ear fused to outer ear.

Figure 3

With right sides together stitch front ears to backs. Notch curved edge, turn right side out and press. (Figure 3). Stitch across raw edge, clip to small ● .

Reinforce body front along upper dart lines pivoting at small ●. Cut along slash line to point. See figure 1. Stitch remaining darts in front pieces, press.

On outside, pin ear to slashed edge of body front, matching dots. (Figure 4).

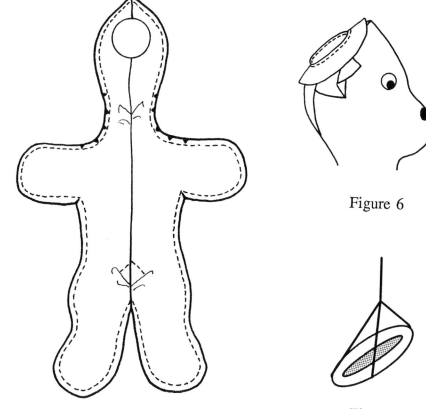

Figure 4

The stitching line of the ear should overlap the stitching line of the dart . Have raw edges even along top of head. Baste. Stitch dart catching all thicknesses.

Figure 6

Figure 5

Figure 7

Stitch body front sections together at center front, matching nose and darts. Clip curves and press. Stitch darts in back body pieces, press. Stitch center back seam matching darts, press.

You are now ready to attach front and back sections . With right sides together stitch around entire bear, clip curves and press. See figure 5. Turn right side out through hole at top. Attach ends of bias strip to form circular shape. With right sides together stitch this bias piece to opening at back of head as shown in figure 6.

Cut 13" length of tubing and form into hoop with dowel as described earlier. Stretch bias strip over this hoop and from the right side "stitch in the ditch" to catch bias on inside. You will want to use a zipper foot for this step and you may have to attach foot after hoop is in place because tubing will not fit under it. After stitching trim off excess bias strip on inside. Because this is a bias edge no seam finish is necessary.

The opening for wind on this windsock is at an angle. Therefore, you will need to tie the strings at uneven lengths as shown. Otherwise, directions on page 5 apply.

Make a bow tie with ribbon and tack at neck to complete this fun little windsock.

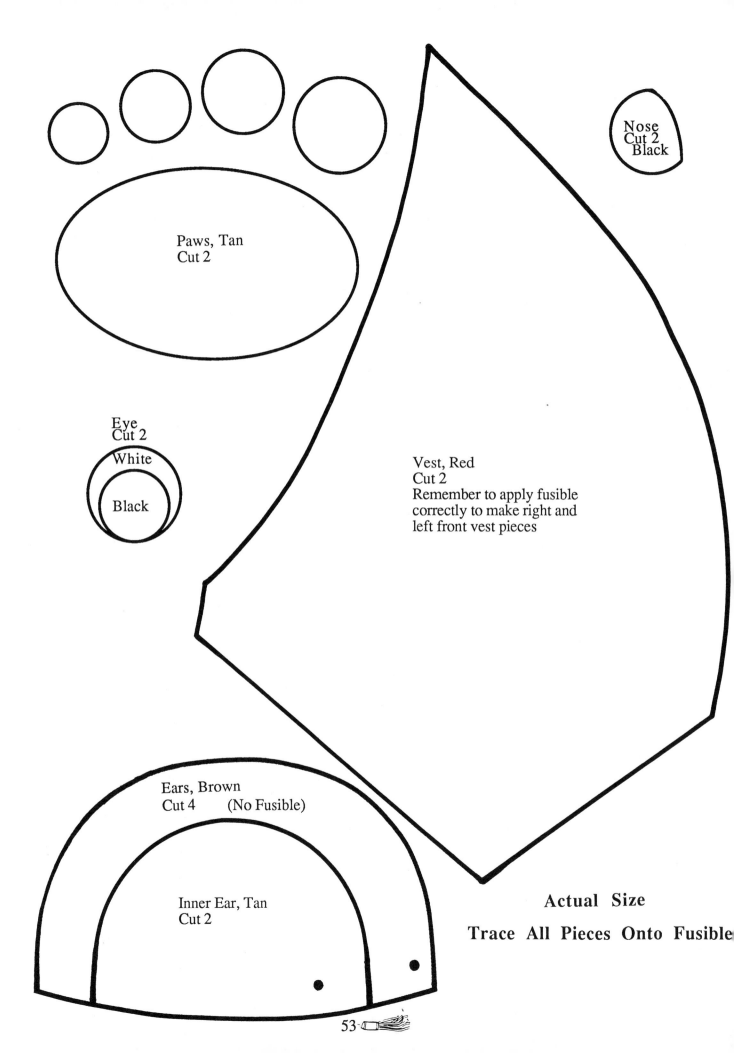

Nose
Cut 2
Black

Paws, Tan
Cut 2

Eye
Cut 2

White

Black

Vest, Red
Cut 2
Remember to apply fusible
correctly to make right and
left front vest pieces

Ears, Brown
Cut 4      (No Fusible)

Inner Ear, Tan
Cut 2

**Actual Size**

**Trace All Pieces Onto Fusible**

53

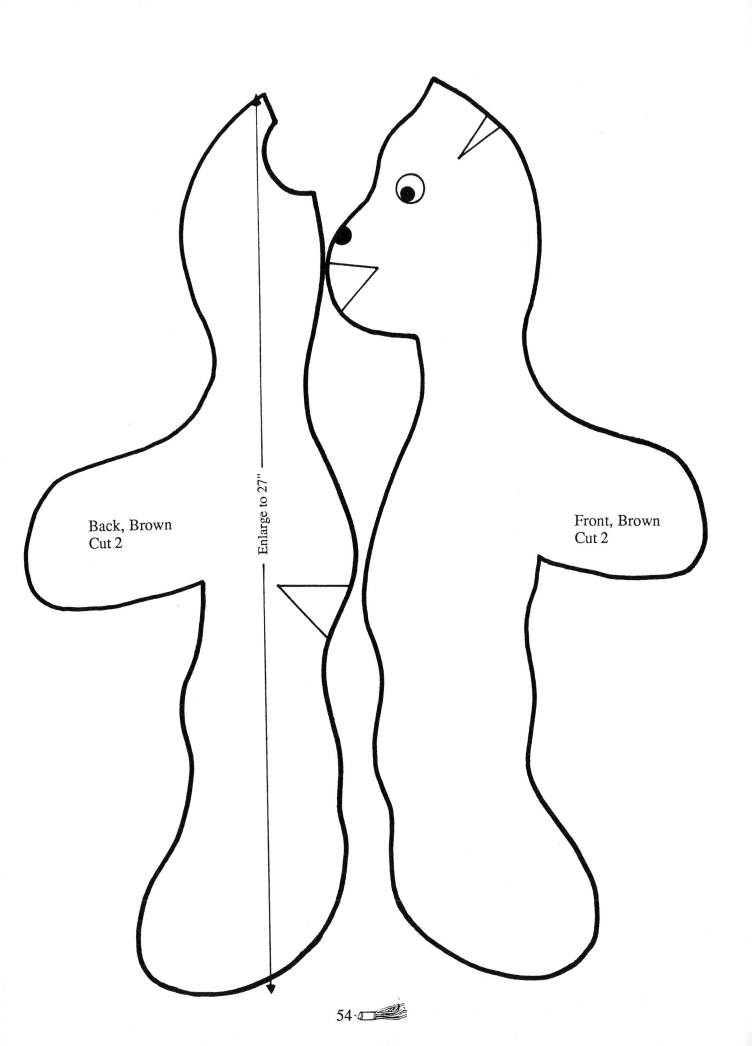

Back, Brown
Cut 2

Enlarge to 27"

Front, Brown
Cut 2

# Miscellaneous Designs
## Totem Pole
### Approximate Length 37 "

After you have made a few windsocks and have a scrap bag of nylon pieces you may want to make this colorful Totem Pole. It is an easy design to make but can be time consuming.

● You will need:

    1/2 yard yellow
    1/8 yard red
    1/8 yard blue
    Various scraps of nylon
    1 yard Wonder Under™
    1/2 yard 1/2" polyester boning
    Matching thread

● Cut:

    2 yellow rectangles, 8 1/4" by 32"
    2 red strips, 1 1/2" by 32"
    1 blue band, 3 1/2" by 17 1/2"
    1 blue band, 4 1/2" by 17 1/2"

● Method:

Enlarge totem pole design to a length of approximately 30". (See page 2). Trace the entire design on Wonder Under™ twice, one for each side of the windsock. Cut the Wonder Under™ apart carefully fusing pieces to different colors. Fuse these pieces to yellow background fabric <u>as you cut them apart</u>. If you cut out all the colorful pieces at once you would have quite a puzzle to put together again. Here is where a big scrap bag of nylon comes in handy. Be creative and have fun making two different totem poles by mixing colors. You can add as much or as little detail to this design as you like. Cut additional small pieces and fuse over larger ones for more detail.

After applying entire design to background pieces  stitch red strips  lengthwise to yellow windsock pieces as shown in figure 1. Finish seams, press. Now add blue bands at top and lower edges of windsock, widest band at lower edge.   Finish these seams, press. See figure 2.

Figure 1

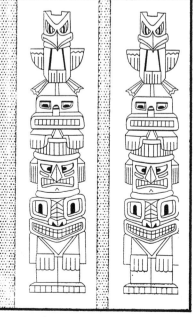

Fold windsock to inside and stitch side seam, finish and press this seam. Turn right side out and by machine make a narrow rolled hem on lower edge. Because this design requires a lot of fusing and added nylon you may find it tends to be stiff and not hang well. To add shaping form an 18" length of boning into circular shape by tacking ends together. Now tack this hoop inside lower edge of windsock to ensure its tubular shape. It is easiest to do all of this tacking by machine. You are now ready to turn to page 5 for final instructions for completing and hanging your Totem Pole windsock.

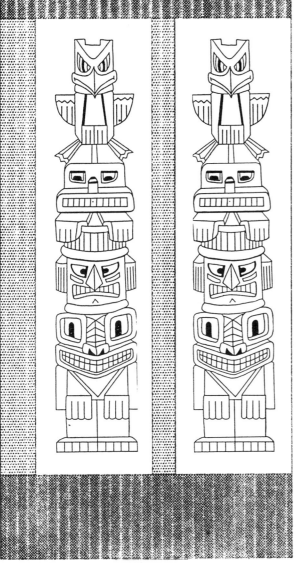

Figure 2

Enlarge to 30"

# Miscellaneous Designs
## Traffic Light
### Approximate Length 52"

Stop traffic with this windsock! The square shape means different finishing techniques but this windsock is still an easy project for the beginner.

● You will need:

    2/3 yard black
    1/4 yard red
    1/4 yard yellow
    1/4 yard green
    1/4 yard Wonder Under™
    Matching thread
    4 dowels, each 1/4" by 5 1/2"

● Cut:

    4 black background pieces,
            6 1/2" by 16"
    2 red streamers, 4" by 38"
    2 green streamers, 4" by 38"
    2 yellow streamers, 4" by 38"
    2 black streamers, 4" by 38"
    On fusible:
        2 red circles
        2 yellow circles
        2 green circles

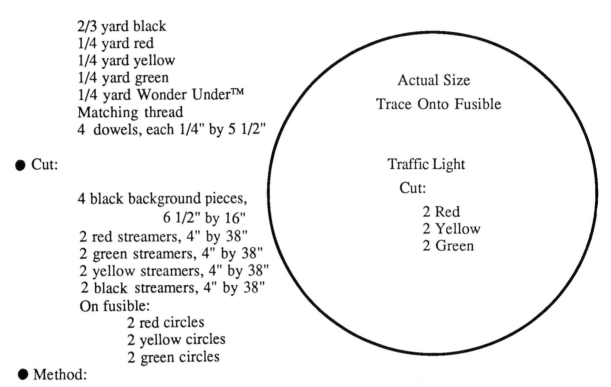

Actual Size
Trace Onto Fusible

Traffic Light
Cut:

    2 Red
    2 Yellow
    2 Green

● Method:

Fuse "lights" to 2 black panels with red on top, then yellow, and green on bottom. Space as shown in figure 1.

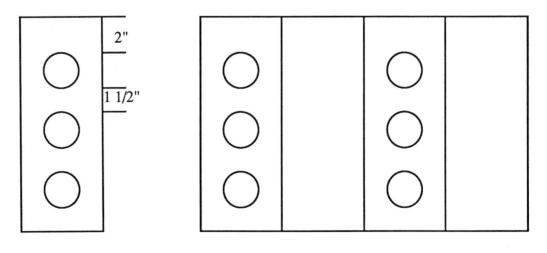

Figure 1

Figure 2

Figure 2 shows all black panels stitched together. Press seams. To give this windsock the square shape you will want to do reverse French seams. Fold on side seams with wrong sides together and re-stitch each seam very close to edge. See figure 3.

Hem long edges and lower edges of all streamers.

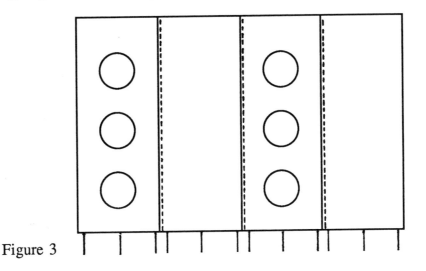

Figure 3

Alternating colors attach streamers to lower edge of windsock spacing 2 per side. Leave a slight gap (1/8") at seams to encourage windsock to retain square shape. (Also shown in figure 3). Remember to leave seam allowance on open edge. Finish seam and press.

Stitch final side seam twice as directed, press. Turn down 1" at upper edge to form casing. Turn raw edge 1/4" to inside and stitch around top leaving openings at diagonal corners for inserting dowels. Dowels work better than tubing in this instance because tubing has been rolled in storage and is hard to straighten completely.

Using black 1/4" twill tape, ribbon or scraps of nylon cut 2, 8" lengths and tack diagonally inside top of windsock to keep it from collapsing in the wind. Tack these stays at casing stitching line so they do not show. See figure 4.

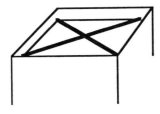

Figure 4

Cut 4 lengths of string each 16" and tie at corners. Finish with knots and swivel as directed on page 5.

# Seasonal Designs
## Uncle Sam
### Approximate Length 43"

"Uncle Sam wants you!" Your neighbors are sure to notice this patriotic windsock. Fly him on July 4th, election day, or any day you want to boast the red, white, and blue.

● You will need:

> 3/4 yard white
> 1/3 yard red
> 1/2 dark blue
> 1/8 light blue
> 1/8 yard black
> 1/4 yard gray
> 1 yard Wonder Under™
> 1/3 yard very stiff interfacing
> Matching thread

● Cut:

Figure 1

> 2 white body pieces, 10" by 31"
> 1 dark blue band, 3" by 19 1/2"
> 2 black bands, 4 1/2" by 10"
> 11 red strips on fusible, 3/4" by 14"
> Cut all other pattern pieces as directed.

● Method:

Begin by constructing hat. Stitch all 16 red and white stripes together to form circular shape for top hat. Finish seams. Fuse stars to dark blue band spacing 3/8" apart and allowing for seam allowance on ends. Stitch side seam of band to make circular shape and with right sides together attach this band to upper portion of top hat as shown in figure 1. Finish seam and press.

To construct hat brim seam outside edge catching both nylon layers plus interfacing. Notch edge. (Figure 2). Turn brim right side out and press. With white thread begin at outer edge and stitch in spiral fashion at 1/4" until you reach inner circle. This will add stability to the brim and keep it from being floppy. (Figure 3).

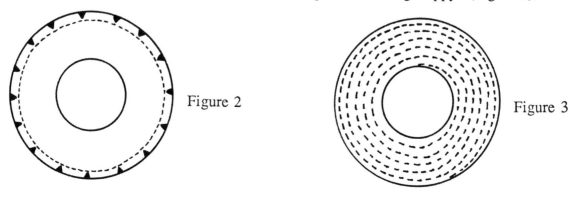

Figure 2                                    Figure 3

With right sides together stitch brim to top portion, finish seam, press and set hat aside.

Fuse all pieces as shown in figure 4. The hair can be added last since it is stitched on, not fused. The beard, however, is fused but only on the top edge so it will flutter in the wind and not entirely cover the bow tie.

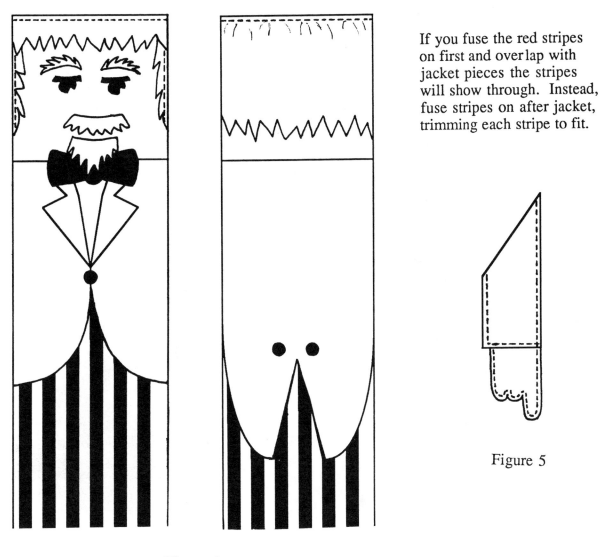

If you fuse the red stripes on first and overlap with jacket pieces the stripes will show through. Instead, fuse stripes on after jacket, trimming each stripe to fit.

Figure 5

Figure 4

Baste hair into place on back (gathering to fit) and baste front hair pieces as shown, also.

Stitch 4 hands to 4 sleeves as shown in figure 5. With right sides together stitch around entire arm leaving open where arm attaches to body. Trim and clip seams. Turn right side out and press. Baste to Uncle Sam's body (figure 6). Attach black bands at lower edges. You are now ready to stitch long side seams, finish and press.

Figure 6

With right sides together stitch hat to top of Uncle Sam's head, finish seam and press.  Make narrow rolled hem on lower edge by machine and then turn to page 5 for final instructions for casing, hoop  and strings.

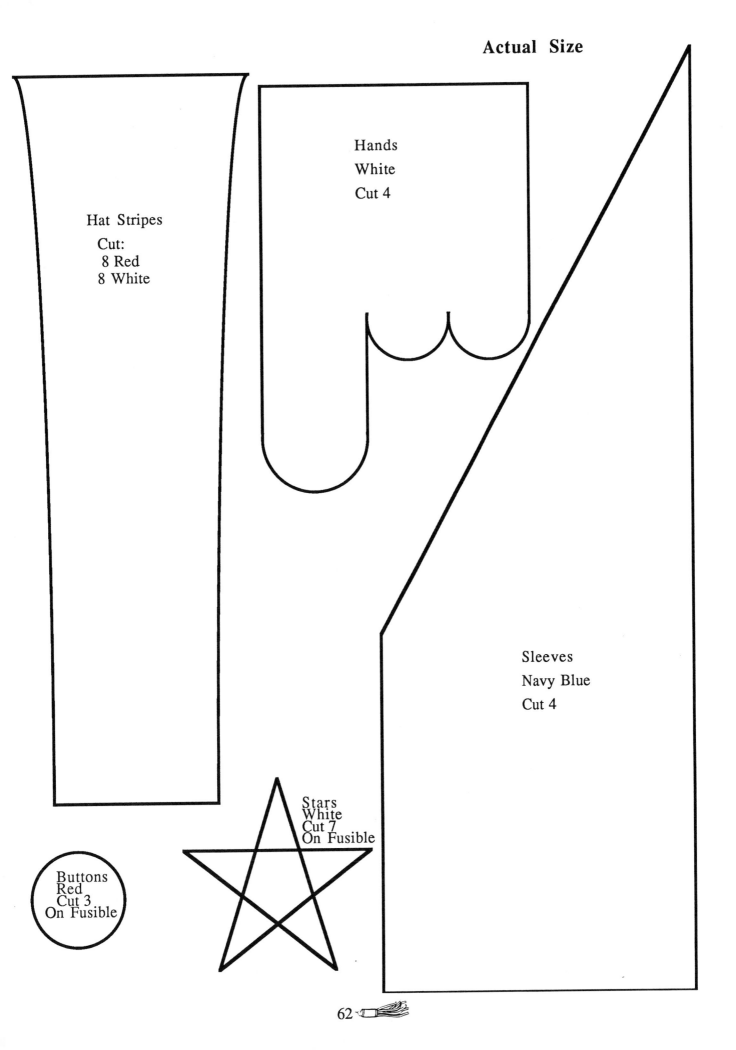

**Actual Size**

Hat Stripes

Cut:
8 Red
8 White

Hands
White
Cut 4

Sleeves
Navy Blue
Cut 4

Stars
White
Cut 7
On Fusible

Buttons
Red
Cut 3
On Fusible

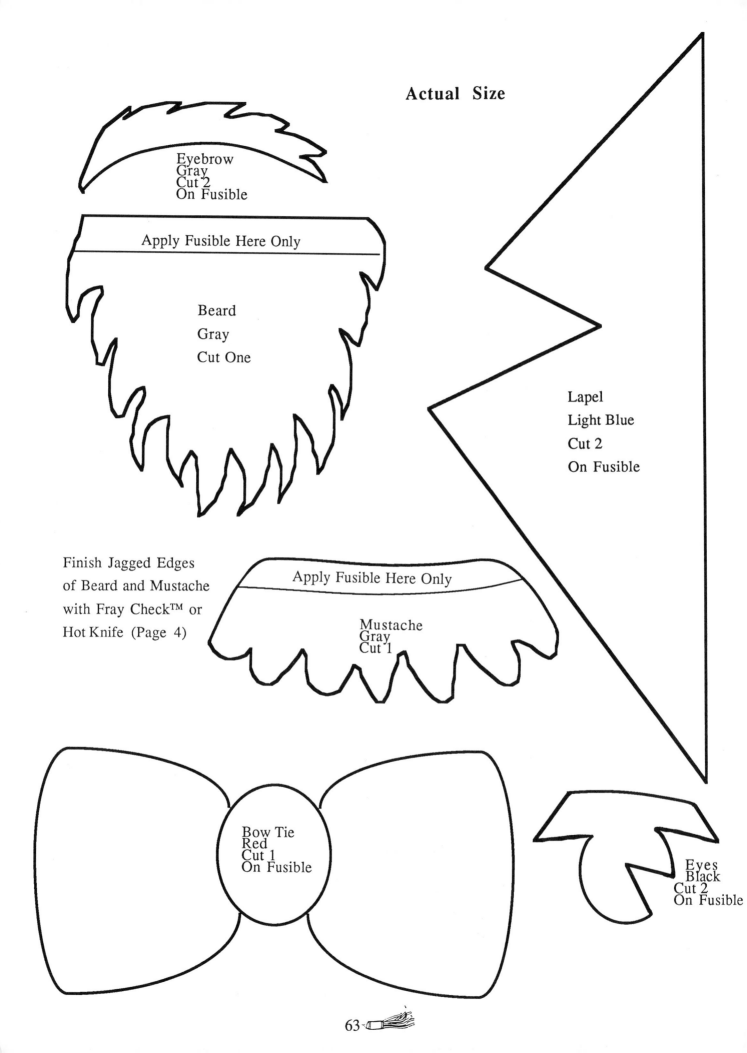

**Actual Size**

Eyebrow
Gray
Cut 2
On Fusible

Apply Fusible Here Only

Beard
Gray
Cut One

Lapel
Light Blue
Cut 2
On Fusible

Finish Jagged Edges
of Beard and Mustache
with Fray Check™ or
Hot Knife (Page 4)

Apply Fusible Here Only

Mustache
Gray
Cut 1

Bow Tie
Red
Cut 1
On Fusible

Eyes
Black
Cut 2
On Fusible

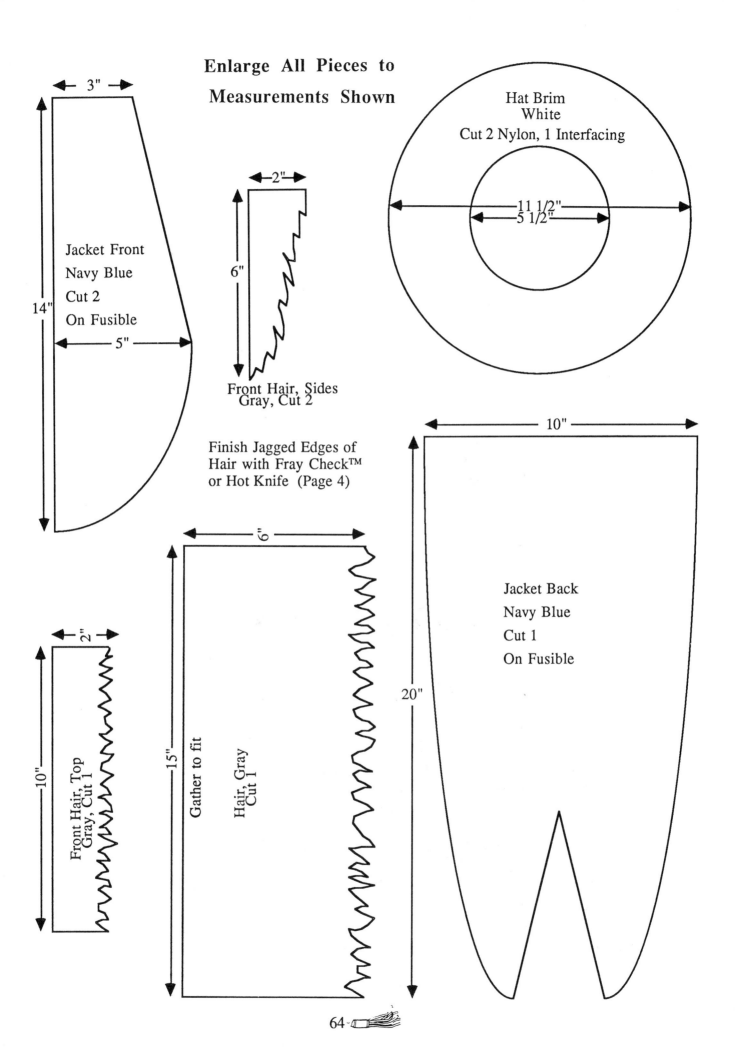

**Enlarge All Pieces to Measurements Shown**

3"

Jacket Front
Navy Blue
Cut 2
On Fusible

14"

5"

2"

6"

Front Hair, Sides
Gray, Cut 2

Finish Jagged Edges of
Hair with Fray Check™
or Hot Knife (Page 4)

Hat Brim
White
Cut 2 Nylon, 1 Interfacing

11 1/2"
5 1/2"

10"

Jacket Back
Navy Blue
Cut 1
On Fusible

20"

2"

10"

Front Hair, Top
Gray, Cut 1

6"

15"

Gather to fit

Hair, Gray
Cut 1

## Seasonal Designs
## Valentine's Day
### Approximate Length 64"

If you have a spot that requires a large windsock you may want to use the dimensions for this one. Also, this heart design will adapt easily if you choose to reduce the size. So get busy and make this windsock for your Valentine, a gift so much more original than flowers or candy.

● You will need:

> 3/4 yard red
> 7/8 yard white
> 1/2 yard Wonder Under™
> Matching thread

● Cut:

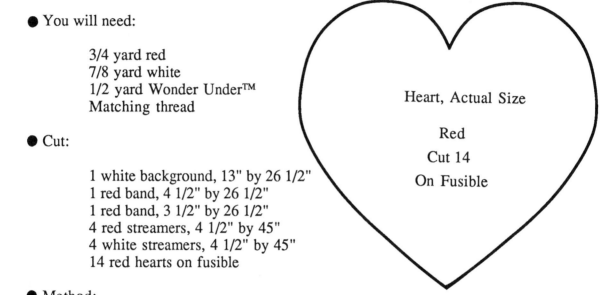

Heart, Actual Size

Red

Cut 14

On Fusible

> 1 white background, 13" by 26 1/2"
> 1 red band, 4 1/2" by 26 1/2"
> 1 red band, 3 1/2" by 26 1/2"
> 4 red streamers, 4 1/2" by 45"
> 4 white streamers, 4 1/2" by 45"
> 14 red hearts on fusible

● Method:

Fuse hearts randomly to white background. Stitch widest red band to top and narrow red band to lower edge as shown in figure 1. Finish seams and press.

Figure 1

Hem long edges and lower edge of all streamers. Turn to page 4 for instructions for attaching them. You are now ready to stitch side seam, finish seam and press. Page 5 gives final instructions for completing your special Valentine.

No, there is nothing wrong with your eyes. These letters are reversed so you can trace directly onto the fusible paper. After applying the letters to your windsock the message will be correct.

69